JOE SILLETT was born at Christ's Hospital School, Horsham in 1972 and was educated there between 1983 and 1990. In 1994, he graduated with a degree in Modern Languages from the University of Manchester. Whilst studying in Manchester, he would regularly watch his beloved Manchester United at Old Trafford, often after having played for the University 1st XI football team on a Wednesday afternoon. A passionate sportsman and fan, he was a season-ticket holder at Girondins de Bordeaux in 1992/3 and later at TSV 1860 Munich. Joe worked for a variety of blue-chip organisations before founding his own sports brand in 2001, which he then ran until October 2008. During this time, he was voted Director of the Month by Director Magazine in the UK. *"Mentality"* is Joe's debut book. The book's website is www.mentality.tv .

KARL MORRIS was born at Christopher Home Hospital, Wigan in 1966. After leaving school, he followed his dream and became a PGA professional golfer. Always passionate about coaching, he developed an extensive level of experience teaching the game at all levels. It became apparent that the 'MIND FACTOR' was an area that was badly represented in sport. Without the constraints of a conventional academic education, he went on to develop outstanding results as a Mind Coach to some of the finest sportsmen and sportswomen in the world. Ashes-winning captain Michael Vaughan, Lee Westwood and Darren Clarke are just a few of the people whom Karl feels fortunate to have worked with on a one-to-one basis. His seminars and workshops have been presented all over the world to diverse groups such as the Australian, Swedish and South African Professional Golf Associations, Manchester United Football Club, the Rugby Football Union and businesses such as Red Bull and Volvo. Karl is the author of 4 books including the 'MIND FACTOR' with Darren Clarke. He has personally tutored a community of 'MIND FACTOR' coaches from over 25 countries. His website is www.golf-brain.com .

CONTACTING THE AUTHORS

If you would like to make direct contact with either Joe or Karl, please use the following e-mail addresses:

joe@mentality.tv   km@golf-brain.com

SPECIAL OLYMPICS GREAT BRITAIN

A percentage of revenue from every book sold is donated to Special Olympics Great Britain.

If you are interested in becoming a coach or volunteer for this charity, then you can find further information on the Special Olympics GB web site: www.sogb.org.uk .

If a friend or member of your family is interested in becoming a Special Olympics athlete, then further information can be found on the Special Olympics GB web site: www.sogb.org.uk .

If you would like to make a separate donation to this charity, then please go to www.justgiving.com/mentality .

Special Olympics GB is a Company Limited by Guarantee and Registered in England and Wales No. 2301452. This company was registered as a Charity in accordance with the Charities Act 1960 No. 800329.

Special Olympics
Great Britain

MENTALITY

First published in Great Britain in 2010 by Joe Sillett and Karl Morris,
The Cottage, Rosier Business Park, Coneyhurst Road, Billingshurst,
West Sussex, RH14 9DE, United Kingdom

Website www.mentality.tv

ISBN 978-0-9564856-0-1

Book design and production by Mike Simister.
mikesimister@yahoo.com

Professional editing by Philip Cunliffe and Christine Barnicoat,
Cunliffe & Barnicoat Media Services Ltd.
www.cunliffeandbarnicoat.co.uk

INTRODUCTION
By Joe Sillett

Every person in the following chapters is a sporting hero. All in their different ways, have fought mentally and physically to fulfil their deepest desire – to be the best. In this book, they describe their passion and pain, challenges and commitment and, above all, unswerving willpower. I feel very privileged to have been able to put this book together and I am deeply grateful to everyone for sharing their stories.

The last decade has taught me how life can be full of highs and lows. After seven years of blood, sweat and tears running my own business, I was made redundant. I had gone full circle from a blank sheet of paper in 2001 (aged 29), to having a business valued at £10million five years later, to then having to sell it in a pre-pack administration deal just two and a half years after that.

It was a whirlwind ride that I look back on with great fondness, and inevitably some sadness. It involved attending some of sport's greatest events and meeting many of my childhood heroes. At its dizziest heights, running the business was exhilarating: Watching the final day of the 2005 Ashes series at the Oval, followed by a night out on the town with the England team. Being a guest at Gary Player's 50th Masters Dinner in Augusta in 2007 and listening to him talk about his approach to life. Playing for the winning team in the 2007 Quinn Direct British Masters Pro-Am golf tournament at the Belfry. As a 17 handicapper, I will never forget the 18th hole. I hit my drive to within 220 yards of the green. I knew I had to carry the lake and make sure my ball didn't end up in the water, so I asked my caddy for the 4-iron, took a deep breath and then hit the best shot of my life to within 10 feet of the pin. My playing partner, Anton Haig, screamed "That was a great shot buddy" and there was a large round of applause from the gallery around the green and people lining the fairway. I simply didn't know where to look – it was a crazy moment and one that I will never forget. In the five seconds or so after my ball rested on the middle tier of the green, I got a small taste of what it must be like to be a professional sportsperson.

Back to January 2009, and being unemployed with a family of three young children was not a good place to be. The recession was at its deepest. I can't remember how many times I sent out my CV, met with recruitment consultants or worked my network, yet nothing tangible arose. I thought back to two of the best books I had ever read before I started my previous venture, and how they had inspired me. Napoleon Hill's *"Think and Grow Rich"* and David J Schwartz's *"The Magic of Thinking Big"*. So I decided to read them again.

When I had met sports people in the past, they always seemed to enjoy talking about their profession. So why not take this a step further and ask them to share their inner thoughts on what it took to reach the top and keep performing at the highest level?

I called Chubby Chandler, Managing Director of International Sports Management, and gave him an outline of the concept. Chubby liked the idea and pointed me towards a charity, Special Olympics Great Britain, where I met Karen Wallin, its CEO in London. Karen told me how its work annually enabled 8,000 athletes with learning disabilities to compete per year and how sport and a competitive environment had enriched the lives of so many people it supports. She also said that the charity doesn't receive a penny from the government, or any backing from the National Lottery. Other than corporate sponsors, the charity is 100% dependent on contributions from members of the public. Here was a charity close to my heart, as my son Sammy was born with Down's Syndrome.

Chubby kindly agreed to give me access to his sports stars and I was told to give Karl Morris, Europe's leading Mind Coach, a call. His wife, Nadine, works for Special Olympics. I talked to Karl about my plans for the book which he found very interesting and he agreed to contribute from an analytical point of view.

For both Karl and me, putting this book together has been an exciting and rewarding experience. Our hope is that this book not only raises money for Special Olympics GB, but that it will have a positive impact on the lives of everyone who reads it.

As the late Vince Lombardi, NFL coach said: *"The difference between a successful person and others is not a lack of strength, not a lack of knowledge, but rather a lack of will."*

His quote would resonate with all of the personalities in this book. All at some point made a commitment to pursue a dream. All reached the top of their chosen sport. All have a different story to tell of how they found success and what this journey was like for them.

CONTENTS

BEN AINSLIE, CBE

Charles Benedict "Ben" Ainslie CBE was born on 5th February 1977 in Macclesfield, Cheshire. He was introduced to the world of sailing aged 4 by his father Roddy. He was educated at Peter Symonds College in Winchester and Truro School in Truro.

His rise through the sailing ranks was swift and meteoric. Now, with three successive Olympic gold medals to his name, he is the most successful British Olympic sailor in history. He was elected ISAF World Sailor of the Year in 1998, 2002 and 2008.

QUESTIONS

As a child, were you good at any other sports and why did you decide to pursue sailing?

Well, sailing really was the only thing - I wasn't very good at anything else! My hand-eye co-ordination isn't fantastic; in fact I only have one eye which works - or focuses properly anyway. I was quite good at cricket and hockey, and played in various school teams. I really enjoyed those sports, but I was never going to be a Freddie Flintoff! Sailing was something I was good at and really enjoyed. When I was aged 10 or 11, I had to make a decision whether I could continue playing in the school cricket team at the same time as sailing. So I made a decision to stick with the sailing, which I think turned out to be the right one.

Your father Roddy had a big influence in introducing you to sailing. Did you have a tutor/pupil relationship in the early days?

Yes, I suppose I was quite lucky because my Dad was a good sailor, albeit in much bigger boats than dinghies, which most kids learn to sail in. Whilst he and my Mum introduced my sister and me to the sport, my Dad encouraged me to try much bigger boats. My Dad didn't really know much about dinghy sailing, so it wasn't a case that he was a pushy father forcing me into bigger boats - he just let me get on with it. I was very fortunate that there was a guy down at my local sailing club called Phil Slater who was a very talented local sailor. He was extremely keen and motivated to teach me and the other kids at the club how to go out there and race. And my Dad wasn't trying to tell me how to do it or what I was doing wrong all the time. He was far more supportive than that.

How old were you when you first thought that you may be able to sail for a living and turn your hobby into a full-time profession?

When I was 18, I won the World Youth Championships and, in the same year, I qualified for the 1996 Olympics. I had an idea that hopefully - if I kept doing well - I could at least dedicate myself to sailing for the next few years. Then, in 2000, I started getting involved in the Americas Cup which career-wise is a good move for a sailor. That, and winning gold at the 2000 Olympics, convinced me that I could make a career in sailing.

How did that work from a funding point of view? Who gave you the money to get your career off the ground?

Prior to 1996, it was always my parents. At that time, there was hardly any funding available for any sports, let alone Olympic sports. But after the 1996 Olympics, that changed, as the National Lottery was established and this has made a huge difference to many sports. Until then though, I was very reliant on support from my parents.

Who was the biggest single influence in helping you be successful?

Without doubt, my Dad. He gave me the financial and emotional support in the early days. There was no way I would have got the results in the early days without that support. Even to this day, it's still great to always have him there if things aren't going well. He provides a bit of common sense, which always helps!

What was the big breakthrough moment in your career?

Winning gold in 2000 was a huge breakthrough. I had won the silver in 1996, which was great for a 19-year-old, but to turn the tables and beat the guy who won gold in 1996 was certainly a defining moment.

What sacrifices have you had to make in order to achieve, and maintain, success?

There are sacrifices in sailing just like any other sport. You have to give up a lot of things which people take for granted, like being at home for any length of time, as you are away from family and friends for long periods. Being at home is a holiday for me – and what I really enjoy most. Jetting off around the world to all these exotic places sounds nice but, in reality, when you are there racing, you're just focused on one thing.

At the start of a season or year, do you set yourself goals and how do you monitor your performance against these goals?

Yes, I always set performance goals. I have long-term goals which generally don't stretch further than 2 to 4 years ahead – and then I set yearly goals as well. I have performance goals in events which I select as those I want – and need - to perform well at. In addition, I have fitness goals and I have financial goals – the amount of money I need to bring in to make it happen. So I set goals in all sorts of different areas of my life which I slowly tick off. Some are much more important than others, some long-term and others are just maybe weekly or monthly ones. But although it's important to try to achieve these, it's not necessarily a total disaster if it doesn't happen. I constantly evaluate my goals.

Do you have a set routine for mentally preparing for an event?

For a race, I definitely do - at the start of each event especially - in terms of what time I leave for the race, for the dock. The pre-start routine and the strategy for the race are very important. All those preparations help to put you mentally in the right frame of mind. Once you've ticked all the boxes and there's nothing more you can do, then it's about just getting on with the racing. This preparation typically lasts for about an hour before the race and slowly gets more defined the closer you get to the start time.

Is there a one-line expression you say to yourself whilst competing to drive you on?

In sailing, the race lasts an hour. It's not like you've got 9.58 seconds these days to get to the other end! It's quite complex with lots of different things happening all the time. You are constantly evaluating the race and what is happening, the strategy and monitoring your work rate so you don't blow yourself up.

Do you think you can control your mind?

That's a really good question. I have never really thought about it that way. To me, it's more about experiences, having been there and done it before and recognising what worked or what didn't work. That's how my mind operates when I'm racing. I think I can probably control my mind better now than when I was younger, and experience helps with that. I wouldn't say I was in total control of my mind though.

Do you ever have doubts or lack of confidence – and, if so, how do you deal with it?

I've been very fortunate. When I'm on land, and not racing, I have the same everyday issues which people do about which parking spot to pick and all those stupid things. I don't know why it is, but when I am racing I have very little doubt. I have a lot of confidence in what I am going to do and I also have the confidence to know that it may not be exactly the right decision - but I know that if it's not the right decision, then I'll be able to come back from that mistake and still be OK.

What do you do when you feel nervous?

I just try to focus on what I need to do; on what I need to do well. I find I am more nervous if the preparation hasn't been right. It's good to have nerves in a way. If you don't have them, then you are probably not taking it seriously enough. Nerves are not a bad thing, but it's about not letting them dominate. Normally though, once you start racing, any nerves disappear and you just get on with it.

How do you deal with extreme pressure?

That's what I really love about the racing I do: the buzz of being under really extreme pressure and having to perform. It's an amazing feeling in a way, what that amount of pressure does to you. I've been fortunate, in most cases, as I have had really good experiences of being under real pressure. In some ways, I get excited by it and look forward to it. But it's important to react to it in the right way, to just use it to stimulate you, to focus more and to work harder and not let it worry you. In my mind, I disassociate myself from the external pressure and just use it as a challenge, enjoying the opportunity of having an extreme challenge, and trying to make the most of it.

Can you give an example of your being at your very best?

Well, I suppose it's in those pressure situations; probably the Sydney Olympics in 2000 is the best example. I had to beat the Brazilian and push him to the back of the fleet. It was an extremely difficult situation to be in and I had to be at my very best in order to do it.

Is there anything you dislike about your sport?

The conditions can make it very difficult for the competitors. There is always an element of luck, of course, although that generally evens out over a series of ten to twelve races. You have to be prepared for adverse weather conditions and you have to be mentally tough to deal with that and to perform well. Bad weather also means that it is not necessarily a spectator-friendly sport. That's often frustrating as well, as it would be nicer if people could understand the sport better. The sport has come a long way in the last 10 to 15 years, though, and we have certainly moved forward in terms of being more TV-friendly. In some ways you could argue that the authorities are trying too hard, because all this media attention is affecting the quality of the racing. It's a very fine line that we need to tread. With modern technology, for instance having more on-board cameras, we are always improving things for the spectator, but you can't do anything about Mother Nature and the winds. That's the biggest issue we've got.

What makes a bad day?

Bad results. Not winning at the end of the series is never great. Not performing. There's nothing more frustrating than making bad mistakes and not performing to your maximum ability.

What's been the lowest point of your career?

After 2000, I spent a year with the US Americas Cup team, which was full of past winners - the top dogs in the Americas Cup – and the top designers, with a huge budget, with a lot of expectation of the team - and for me, as it was my first exposure to the Americas Cup. I was very young – too young - and on my own, so after a year I decided to go back to Olympic sailing. But at the time, as I walked away from the Americas Cup team, I wondered whether that could be the end of my sailing career - it's a small community and a small world and walking away from a team like that was quite a big gamble. Fortunately, it turned out to be the best thing I ever did. I didn't know that at the time. It was a pretty low time, scary in a way.

So how did you bounce back from that?

I got back into Olympics sailing almost immediately, changed classes and four months later won the World Championships in that new class. That was probably one of the happiest days of my life, as I realised that I hadn't completely lost it as a sailor. I'd pulled myself back, which was a huge relief.

What's been the most important ingredient in your achieving success?

I think determination is crucial - doing what it takes to succeed. I suppose it's the same in every sport - sometimes it looks very easy but, behind the scenes, there's a lot of hard work and effort which goes into being successful.

How do you continue to motivate yourself when you've won three successive Olympic gold medals?

We're lucky in sailing in that there's a lot of different challenges out there. There's the Americas Cup and Round The World Ocean racing - so for me, especially at the moment, I can back off Olympic sailing and focus on the Americas Cup and other types of sailing, which continues to increase my knowledge and experience, but at the same time, when I get back to the Olympic sailing, I'm that much fresher and motivated to go out there and train. Of course, you always have to come down from a peak, but normally I have found that you can get back up to an even higher peak next time.

Do you have a roadmap to retirement?

In terms of Olympic sailing, I'll be 35-years-old in 2012 and Olympic sailing is physically very demanding. So, if I can qualify and do well, that would be a perfect opportunity to call it a day.

Is there anything you would do differently if you had your time again?

I probably wouldn't have been in such a rush all the time! I think I've always wanted to get to the next level as fast as I can. In 2000, I wanted to get involved in the Americas Cup and perhaps I did that too quickly, without the right support and network behind me, with the wrong team. So I suppose I'd slow down a bit and not be in quite a rush to move on.

If there was one piece of advice that helped you become successful, what was it?

I was told very early on never to give up. It's obvious of course but it is advice that has served me well over the years. However, the most important thing which I have learnt in my sporting career so far is honesty, especially within yourself – honesty in terms of analysing your performance and what you need to do better as a performer.

What one-line sentence would you give to anybody aspiring to be the best they could be?

You have to be 100% in every area. In some ways, you have to be ruthless to achieve that.

Which sportsman or sportswoman from another sport do you admire the most and why?

I really admire Tiger Woods. There are quite a lot of similarities between golf and sailing, in terms of the psychological challenges. It's not quite as long for each race compared to a round of golf, but certainly the weather can be a major factor and there are lots of highs and lows. You can see Tiger's focus is that much sharper than the other guys and quite often that's what pulls him through.

KARL MORRIS SUMMARY

One of the first things that strikes me about Ben Ainslie's story and what we can all learn from it, is the relationship with his father. It is very obvious there is a deep respect and sense of gratitude here for the help and sacrifice his father has given. Most importantly, though, it is obvious Ben's father gave support and encouragement but he didn't cross the line to the point of parental obsession and interference. He was strong enough to support him and smart enough to know when it was appropriate for Ben to be coached by others.

One of the most disturbing aspects of being involved in top-class sport these days is what I see as an ever-increasing number of parents leading a 'second life' through the exploits of their children in the sporting arena. Very often this parental domination can, in the short term, produce results but it does tend to create a long-term problem for the boy or girl if they are put under too much pressure to succeed. The love of the game for its own sake must never be lost.

Ben Ainslie

As is clear with Ben Ainslie, we must make sure as parents that we do not create a sense of self in a child which is just dependent on sporting results and numbers.

The most successful British Olympic sailor of all time lets us know quite clearly that if we want to become the very best that we can be, we must accept certain sacrifices will have to be made.

As part of our genetic make-up as human beings, we all have a section of our brain which wants INSTANT gratification. We want success now, here, today.

Yet, things clearly do not work that way in the world of sport. You have to be in it for the long haul. You have to be prepared to invest time now without the certainty of a pay-off later.

It is fascinating to read that Ben loves 'the feeling' of pressure. The thrill of competition. This again is so important as to HOW we represent things in our mind. It is so easy to get caught up in media phrases like a 'life-and-death' situation when it comes to winning at sport. Winning or losing is NOT life or death. However, if that is the way you represent a situation to your brain, do you think you are going to feel nervous?

It is clear Ben Ainslie relishes these situations as an OPPORTUNITY to express himself in his chosen arena. The 'feelings' of nervousness in his body he channels by being excited about the chance to compete. It is never framed as life or death. Clearly, he also understands that if all his preparation boxes are ticked, he has given himself the best opportunity to succeed.

JOHN AMAECHI

John Ekwugha Amaechi was born on the 26th November 1970 in Boston, USA to a Nigerian father and an English mother. At the age of 4, his mother brought him to Manchester, UK to escape from his father. He was educated at Stockport Grammar School. By the age of 10, he was 6ft but not only was he tall, he was also overweight. Aged 17, and standing 6ft 8 inches, Amaechi was stopped on Market Street in Manchester by two basketball coaches who asked him if he'd like to try the sport. Although he'd never touched a basketball, within six years from that day, he was playing for the Cleveland Cavaliers in America as a 23-year-old rookie centre, the first undrafted agent to make the starting line-up in the history of the National Basketball Association.

His career took him to Europe where he played for Panathanaikos in Greece and Kinder Bologna in Italy. In 1999, he signed for Orlando Magic in the NBA. In 2000, Amaechi turned down a $17-million, six-year contract with the LA Lakers to stay with Orlando Magic for $600,000 per year. In 2001, he signed for Utah Jazz where he played for three years before being traded to the Houston Rockets. He never played for Houston and retired from the game shortly afterwards. He is now a psychologist and social entrepreneur working in both the United States and Europe. He is also an ambassador for Special Olympics Great Britain.

QUESTIONS

You had an incredibly difficult childhood. You were unusually tall and, by your own admission, out of shape. You were ribbed at school and life was tough. You missed swimming classes at school as you feared them too much. Would it be fair to say that because of your size and weight, you had little or no interest in sport whatsoever?

I don't know if it was because of my size, but it certainly didn't help. It contributed enough to my own ever-increasing body dysmorphia – the idea that I was hideous. For me, sport involved so many things that were contrary to who I felt I was. I knew I was fat and out of shape – and that out-of-shape people don't play sport. I certainly didn't want to have to show myself up next to people who were in shape, because it highlighted how horrible I was. I was also put off by the way sport was coached as well. The idea that every fallibility that a person has is exploited by a coach who has a Napoleon syndrome. That was my early experience of sport which turned me off it from the start.

What do you remember of the day when you were approached in the street in Manchester and asked whether you would like to have a go at playing basketball?

Not much to be honest. For one of those pivotal moments, when a person's universe splits, it has left remarkably little residue. All I remember is being approached by two people, them asking me if I wanted to play basketball, me saying yes and then an overall feeling of confusion, because the meeting was then over. They didn't take my number, I wasn't in school uniform, I don't remember telling them that

I went to Stockport Grammar School and yet two weeks later, I got a message through the office at the school telling me where I could play basketball. I went down and off I went.

Where previously you had felt very uncomfortable competing at any sport, you immediately found a new "home" on the basketball court. This really was a defining period in your life. Your confidence levels on and off the court started to rise sharply. Just how liberating was this whole new world you found yourself in?

Psychologically, it was an amazing discovery. The reality is it is like believing you are the only one of something and then discovering that there is a whole group of people just like you. I thought I was the only person who had to deal with stupid people making comments about my height or my feet or whatever else – and then I entered a room and was surrounded by people just like me. It was lovely. And it was the first time that people saw potential in me. Instead of looking at me and thinking "Oh no, how are we going to fit him in?", I just fitted right in. Rugby was always a challenge because they couldn't fit me in the second row, so I had to play number 8 and I wasn't fast enough to be a number 8. Whereas with basketball, I just fitted. My skills weren't up to the requisite standard of course, but people saw the potential for me to become brilliant and that was highly important.

Who was the biggest influence in helping you make this dramatic turnaround?

The biggest influence on an ongoing basis was my mother, who always showed remarkable confidence in me to do anything that I put my mind to. And also my coach, Joe Forber, who is actually still the head of my Basketball Centre. He was very instrumental, just because his style was such that I never wanted to disappoint him. He wasn't the first coach I had, but he was certainly the most important person who kicked off my career.

One day, aged 17, out of the blue you announced to your mother that you would like to play in the National Basketball Association. With her encouragement, you sat down and wrote "The Plan". Looking back, how important was it to have a document that would chart all of the necessary steps you needed to make to achieve your dream?

Having some tangible thing, whether it's a written document or a well-conceived idea in your head, is essential for achieving great things. To be moderately successful, one can wander a little bit in the wilderness and occasionally come across something good. But to be consistently great, it requires the type of focus that means that every time a crossroads is approached, you know as you come to it what your options are and you know where each of those options will lead. You certainly know if any of those options will lead you down a blind alley. For me, having "The Plan" meant that I didn't know the right decision to make at all times, but I knew how to evaluate the consequences. I knew how to do the meta-thinking. There was never a circumstance which came up which I had never considered. I could never be surprised because I had considered it at some point, not always in huge detail, but it had always been a part of my process. Getting to the NBA was not what I thought it would be, not at all – both in good ways and in plenty of bad ways. One of the first steps in "The Plan" was introspection. It's the step that everybody misses when they set goals. When setting goals, you must remember that people imagine you as a complete finished product, but it's your interaction with the world that forms part of that plan. Part of "The Plan" was knowing my limitations. I knew I was essentially lazy. Now I'm retired, I don't exercise. I don't enjoy it, my body hurts a lot (I'm having surgery this year). But if I was healthy, I still wouldn't because I don't enjoy it and I am not being paid to do it. There are my motivators. I know what they are. When I started playing in the NBA, I relocated my house; I built a house 5 miles away from the trainer I had selected. A trainer I knew I could work well with, because I knew his personality and he knew what I was like. I arranged everything so that I never got out of shape. That's the beauty of a plan that takes into account who you are, as well as these outside factors.

How daunting and difficult was it for you to go about executing this plan and how often did you think you were close to failing?

I think the fear of being close to failing is what helped greatly. I always knew that when I went to America for the first time, Mum had put up 1,000 dollars for plane-flights, food, paying a little bit to the family who was looking after me and that was it. That was all we had. If I didn't get a scholarship for the next year, it was over. It was very clear. There was a set of criteria and a line of demarcation – if I did not pass this line, ie getting a paid, full, college scholarship, then it was over. That really does focus your mind. When someone comes to you on a Friday night and says we're all going to go out and get hammered, and you've got a game the next day, it's not just a question of maybe I won't be as good in the game tomorrow, it's a question of I know that scouts will be at the game, I know that I haven't reached this line, and it's very clear. When I didn't get drafted to the NBA, and many other moments where I felt it was all going to be over, that I'd wasted all this time, I felt devastated. Yet at the same time, that helped to keep me motivated.

How many moments were there of "I'm not going to make it"?

In my first three years in America, pretty much every week was a crisis of confidence. My first year was all about signing my first college scholarship. Then I went to Vanderbilt University but that didn't work out. So I had to sign another college scholarship and that whole year I couldn't play and it was very difficult to just watch and practise and not participate. That happened for three years every week and, beyond that, it seemed like every couple of months there'd be something that happened, a lockout perhaps. There was always something there to challenge you.

What was your big breakthrough moment?

In terms of basketball, it has to be the day that I made it to the Cleveland Cavaliers. That wasn't my best playing epoch, it wasn't the period of time where I did the best in sport, but the process is brutal. As an unsigned, undrafted free agent, to enter a camp with 28 other guys vying for 3 spots was remarkably difficult. They are all doing the same thing you are doing. They've all had the same advice from their agents, and nearly all of them were better athletes than I was. Every day we walked into the locker room and they would pull off one of those name labels, and it was "is it me today?" But the day that the guy came in, pulled it off and put in my name plate in bronze, I knew I had made it.

How did you convince yourself that you were one of the three out of twenty-eight to get through?

It was all about preparation. I spent the entire summer and 45,000 dollars I didn't have, getting into debt, paying to live in this one-bedroom apartment which was full of scorpions and cockroaches, literally next door to where I trained. I'd roll out of bed at 6am, train, come back at 10am, roll into bed, roll out of bed again and then at noon go out and train again, roll back in. That was my routine. By the time I got to the Cleveland camp, I was in unbelievable shape. I was just - ready. I'd taken 2,000 jump shots every day. I'd dribbled the ball every day. I'd run every day. I didn't even think about being one of the three until they started pulling names off. It wasn't a question of thinking it was a foregone conclusion, it was a question of thinking I've done every single thing that I can. There are no extraneous points within my control. Again, the big part of "The Plan" was knowing what I could control. I controlled my nutrition – just a teaspoonful of honey on top of a piece of rye bread in the morning before I went to training, because too much and I would be sick from all of the running. My preparation was meticulous. I got the best trainer I could afford (or rather couldn't afford!) and I did everything I could so it was a question of going in with great peace of mind knowing that anything that happened was out of my control.

What sacrifices have you had to make in order to achieve success?

Too many. There are two types of people who achieve great things. There are people for whom the goal means everything and therefore achieving the goal is the goal. And there are people who want to kick people's arses (and I fall into this second category). I just like to beat people at things. It doesn't matter whether I am giving a speech and I know I have an entire audience of 5,000 people in the palm of my hand, or when I'm teaching or when I am working as a psychologist. Whatever it may be, I just like to know that I am brilliant. I sacrificed an awful lot in terms my personal life, being away from my family, living in a foreign country (there were lots of good things about that also of course) and, in the end, putting a ball into a hoop just doesn't mean that much to me. In my house, there's a remarkable lack of basketball paraphernalia. I don't have that stuff because it's just not that meaningful to me. The reality is that doing what I did doesn't mean that much to me. I know it's important in the scheme of things, I know what I have achieved is significant, but the sport itself is not that meaningful to me.

That's an incredible thing to say for someone who has shed the blood, sweat, tears and man hours you have in basketball?

I was the first basketball player from Britain to make it in America and the very best. That's cool and that's a good thing. That'll do.

If there was one piece of advice that helped you become successful, what was it?

I honestly believe that the root of greatness is in knowing yourself well – something my Mum instilled in me from the start. If you know yourself well, you can never be ambushed by people, or by information about yourself. And you can never run out of petrol, as you always know how much you have in the tank. You always know what bits of you are available and will be needed for any given task - and whether you have that resource available. Even as those things fluctuate, knowing yourself is immensely valuable. The other piece of advice I was given was by my coach, Joe Forber. After I had been playing basketball for a little bit, he asked me when I was going to take it seriously. That was like a switch being flicked. There is an element for people who undertake activities, whether they are in business, sport or anything else, that they are "playing" at them. I don't watch X *Factor*, but you see it on shows like that. You can tell people who are playing at it and if they move forward, they are really pleased, and if they move forward on their raw talent, it makes them really happy. But the people who are enduringly successful are not playing at it, they are not dabbling, they are not getting by on their physical or otherwise talents, they are actually self-propelled, moving forward not at other people's whims, but by controlling everything they can and there's a massive difference in these two mindsets. I don't know that I changed my behaviour radically when I decided this, but it does change things when you stop thinking - wouldn't it be nice to be a millionaire? - wouldn't it be nice to be a sportsman? - wouldn't it be nice to be a singer? – to thinking, I am going to be a singer and this is how I do that. I think that is the difference.

Did you have a set routine for mentally preparing before each game?

Yes, it's vital to be able to prepare in lots of different environments. You have to be able to adapt. If you have a very rigid scheme which involves lots of external elements, then you're going to be in trouble. Or you'll do what a lot of sportspeople do, they play differently at home than they do away. You'll notice this from them because they have a different set of preparations. I actually had the reverse when I played in the NBA. For my first six months, the stats were kept and the assistant-coach came up to me and said "I don't understand, are you doing something different on the road than you do at home, because you are playing better on the road than you do at home?" We didn't come up with anything specific, but just having that conversation made me aware of the deficit. The way that the NBA keeps stats is very specific. We're talking a 3% difference in the output in scoring, a 4% difference in rebounds, things like that. Being aware of it made me very mindful of it when I played. I started to build up a set of expectations from my home fans. Orlando started talking about me. People started to say that I wasn't just some reject, but really good. And yet, I went on the road and people had a different picture of me – so there were no expectations and I could kick their arse until the next time I came back. There was never any pressure. My structure for preparing involved tea and music. Being able to isolate yourself and to give yourself a moment in your own head is a really valuable thing. Some people call it meditation, but whatever it is, being able to spend a little moment inside your head to calm yourself is immensely valuable. I never make a task or a game or whatever it may be last a whole day. So I never woke up in the morning and thought I've got a game today. You have to be able to turn it on, and you have to be able to dial it down again because you can't sustain it for a long period of time. Especially if you are a businessperson working five days a week for 48 weeks a year, you just can't sustain that kind of elite level. When I was playing basketball, I would usually allow myself a lie-in. Then we would have a shoot around in the morning. We'd go through some stretching – and in that process of stretching, I'm thinking of nothing but the stretching. It's about practising, focusing on whatever we were running through, focusing again...then it's done, getting back home, resting, then it's getting back in for the game. And in the car-ride on the way, my kids -

who were with me by that time - would know that that was not the
time to talk to me. That was the time that I was starting to prepare for
the game. Afterwards, we would go to the gym, go through the same
routines, the same people would be in front of me. You just incorporate
them. Walking through, the security guy grabs your hand and says
hello. The guy who takes your car takes your car and says hello. So it
all builds on this routine as you walk through the arena doors. And on
the road, you can do the very same thing. So much so that on the road,
I had ball boys from opposing teams that brought me tea before games,
because they knew that that was part of my thing. It didn't help their
team, but it helped me!

Do you think you can control your mind?

Yes, but we all have a limited capacity to control our mind because
there's so much of it that we do not understand about how it works. A
big part of controlling your mind is controlling your emotions,
controlling rogue thoughts, because they make the mind into a morass.
You have to have coherent thoughts in the middle of all this other stuff.
Having tinnitus going on around your brain is almost impossible.
What I am very good at is extracting the noise, getting rid of it and
having single coherent thoughts. I can't do it all the time, but just like
when I was playing, when it's on, it's on.

How do you deal with doubt?

I think doubt is important. If you're introspective at all, doubt is very
informative. If you know yourself, doubt is informative.

What do you do when you feel nervous?

As a sportsperson, I did all the things which most sportspeople do –
which is bravado: you externalise your nervousness and turn it into
something else. For the most part, I thought that it was a signal, as I am
quite analytical generally and I know that biologically speaking, it's a
signal that you are about to release massive amounts of adrenalin and,
to use old-fashioned terminology, you are in a fight or flight-mode, and
it means you are preparing, so it is something you should embrace. I
can't remember when I played ever being on the court and thinking I
just don't want to do this, I'm overmanned here, there's nothing I can
do. So the nerves never got to a point where they incapacitated me. I

know it does with some people. But I think a lot of that is the fact that people do not look at themselves or their environment in a realistic way. They look at standing in front of a crowd of people as if these are people with spears and stones who would kill them if they make a mistake. That kind of dissonant thinking is what creates the overrun of nerves.

What is the best example of you being at your very best?

When I played in Orlando, we got to the point very quickly where I didn't think I could miss. And even now - and I don't shoot a basketball very often - I am literally surprised if I miss. It's hard to describe. I know I miss 50% of my shots like all basketball players, even the great ones, but it is rare that I take a shot and I think it's going in and it misses. And if it does, I want to examine how that is even possible. I even say it out loud sometimes. I know what I was thinking when I shot it. I know how my arm was positioned. And normally you can feel if it is just not right. I went through a period in Orlando where I would score 10 points of my 15 points a game in the first quarter. And my team would always go to me in that first quarter. The opponents knew that I would be getting the ball on the left block, I knew it, my teammates knew it, and I would still score and there'd be nothing anyone could do about it. That was a good time.

When you have achieved a certain level of success, how easy is it to take your eye off the ball and believe the hype around you?

It is easy to do. It's just remarkable that you can show the skills and the capacity to get to that level, and for those skills and processes to degenerate so quickly. I never once thought that if I stopped practising, the ball would still go in the hoop - never - but there are people who think that. They get to a level and think all they need to do is coast. It's remarkable that anyone would think that the processes that get you to the heights would then change. It's like you get halfway up Everest, and because you are halfway there, you don't need the crampons any more. I don't understand that. To me, the people who fail like that are just moseying along on their talent alone. They are playing at it and because of their physical or innate abilities are managing to hang in there quite comfortably. These are the people who fail most readily at the top. If you've really had to work at it, you don't fail when you get to the top.

When setting goals, how important is it to take one step at a time and do what you can in the moment?

It is important to set achievable goals. It's quite old-fashioned thinking, setting short-term, medium-term, long-term goals. What's more modern, and really necessary in terms of motivation, are two things: that in-built knowledge of who you are and the skills at your disposal, and a vivid moving picture, a future history if you like, of what you are aiming for. A lot of young people play football. When you ask them about football, what they really want is to be rich and to have Cheryl Cole as their girlfriend. What they really want is fame and adulation. These things are not the same as being a footballer: these are just the trappings of football. What they are aiming for is not football, so they are already heading in the wrong direction. You may get to a certain point, and think, do I really have to practise twice a day? To play a game every week with all the travel is boring and monotonous. All these things will mount up, because you are unaware of them. The money which was involved in basketball, the idea of being famous and being looked at and pointed at were for me, a fat and tall 17-year-old kid, not why I wanted to be a player. I wanted to play on a regular basis against some guy who had played basketball since he was two and then I would kick his arse. That's what I wanted. I wanted to do it in America because that's where the best people played. That was how clear and focused I was. Right from the beginning, from the age of 17, I could see myself on the floor with Larry Bird and Magic Johnson, whenever I thought about where I was going.

You went from being an overweight youth to one of the top 300 basketball players in the world. What advice would you give to someone who finds themselves in a similarly difficult phase of their life?

I honestly think you have to be open to these tangential ideas. From the age of 8, I knew I would be a psychologist. Playing basketball involved so many aspects that I didn't think I would be comfortable with – for example, running, sweating – and yet at the same time I saw an opportunity in it. I saw the possibility of becoming really good at something unexpected. I think you have to be prepared to grasp these opportunities and take a chance. All life is risk. Part of what makes reward sweeter, even if not greater, is the fact that you have risked a lot to get there. Open your eyes inside first, that's what I would say. If you are in a position where you feel like you are in a dead end, you're in a rut, whether that's your father's or your mother's rut, or your science teacher's rut, or your Headmaster's rut, or the rut that comes with the area you live in, or your gender or your race. If you are in some kind of rut that you think is not you, you have to know who you are first and then move from that place.

You mention your sexuality in your book. How difficult was it to overcome the problems that this presented you with as a basketball player?

I think the major problem is that you are alone. Even when you are with people, you are alone. If you are with people who don't know who you are, or more accurately for some of my teammates who don't really want to talk about who you are, then you are alone. Also there is a performance edge to this which is something I explore a lot in the work that I do, in that it's very difficult to be brilliant at something when there is an element of your life that makes you feel less than good about yourself. It's also very difficult if every time you are engaged with your performance group, whether it be a team or management team, you are always marking off a section of your energy to stop you from making a mistake interpersonally – such as not talking about when you went to the cinema with some bloke, or not using the wrong pronoun when talking about people. If you are using energy for that, when it comes to the elite edge, whether it be business or sport, when we know the difference between first and forgotten are these tiny increments, then that energy is the difference. So for me, it added to the burden.

What's been the most important ingredient in your achieving success?

I'm highly contra-suggestive. I'm very arrogant and I like to beat people at things. It is a combination of these three things. It's a horrible part of my personality. I never wanted to just win, I wanted to beat people and there is a big difference. I'm not interested in just winning, I want to punish you. I want to make you feel embarrassed. I want to devastate you psychologically and emotionally if we play and that's quite ruthless. As a psychologist, you do this differently. I gain pleasure now from the fact that when I am with someone, I can assess them really well and I can help them with their problem very cleverly and very quickly. It's a different type of kicking someone's arse. It's not the kind of "I got you" mentality; you don't do it that way.

What would you do differently if you had your time again?

From a selfish point of view, I just wouldn't play basketball. I'd be a psychologist probably working in London somewhere, as I do now. I can't imagine it looking very different visually from what I am doing now. I would hope to have a family (I've had a family), but I would hope to have another family. I probably wouldn't be so jaded.

What is the secret to achieving a dream?

The secret to achieving anything extraordinary is helping people to understand the difference between a mythical outcome and a mythical process. I remember playing at Fog Lane Park in Manchester, and people were saying I was just a fat kid from Stockport who only started playing six weeks ago. I distinctly remember those things being said. But people have these mythical outcomes all the time and picture in their minds the things they want to do: play in the NBA, be an astronaut, play in the Premiership for Manchester United. These are mythical outcomes and they are absolutely essential for achieving extraordinary things. You don't get to be Richard Branson by wanting to own the corner shop. You have to see the big picture. The problem is people have these mythical outcomes and because of this they think that the process to get there is somehow mythical also. That it's ethereal, it just kind of happens. People get this idea that if they want it badly enough, it will happen. That is a corollary – it correlates with success but it isn't a causal thing for success. You really want it, yes, that's parallel – but that's not why you get it. People don't get things just because they really want them. I really want my car payment to be half what it is, but that's not what's going to make it happen. There's also this ethereal element between now and this massive mythical thing. The secret to achieving mythical outcomes is having the most well thought-out, pragmatic understanding of yourself which then informs a well thought-out pragmatic plan to get where you want to be.

So at what point should people close to you be prepared to tell you that you may not get there?

It's important to have experts who tell you that. Parents tend to want to avoid sending their children into situations where they will be disappointed or hurt. That is part of the role of a parent - and it's a good role. That's why parents shouldn't try and inform their son or daughter who is good at physics and astronomy, but not so good physically, that they can't be an athlete, just because they look at them as puny and unathletic. That's not their role. Their role is to support their child. If the Head of the British Space Programme comes along and says sorry, you have a spinal problem and therefore cannot be an astronaut, that's different. My son Chris came to me and asked me if basketball was going to be his thing. I remember this because he was in college playing basketball, and he'd really invested in it, but he also had a serious girlfriend and lots of other things going on for him. That was the day he was asking me to kill him – and I said no I don't think it is – and he said he wanted to hear it from someone who knew. Now that's a different role. Yes I was his father, but it's a different role. However, it's good to have naysayers, people on the periphery who tell you that you can't, because they are hecklers, and you learn through hecklers.

What one-line sentence would you give to anybody aspiring to be the best they could be?

People are multi-dimensional. Whilst most really successful people decide on one dimension to focus on, excellence spills over. If you want to be great at one thing, you have to be willing to expand all of your horizons and head in every direction. For people wanting to be extraordinary, you have to be willing to focus on your whole self, not just that one direction that you are heading in. You can't be a successful sportsperson who then ignores everything else about themselves: education, family, morals. Whatever else, these are aspects that cannot be ignored.

Which sportsman or sportswoman from another sport do you admire the most and why?

I like Martina Navratilova. She's a good friend and is, I think, remarkable in what she has achieved. And also Daley Thompson. He seemed a gentleman. He decided to be this elite athlete and I heard him when he spoke to the camera. I heard him when he spoke to children. I saw him when he did events. He was this rounded person who hadn't forgotten that there was more to being human than being elite.

KARL MORRIS SUMMARY

It is very clear John has been extremely successful against all the odds in a world that he didn't even know existed until a relatively late age. Not only has John been outstandingly successful, but he clearly understands what the ingredients to success are for him personally. His naturally introspective nature has allowed him to give us an incredible amount of priceless information on the route-map to success.

What I think is perhaps the most useful advice from John is having the 'self-knowledge' to be able to understand and take into account our own weaknesses. As he quite rightly states, setting goals and 'wanting it badly' are just not enough to create the conditions for success.

Which areas are you weak in? Where do you let yourself down? John realised by his own admission he was naturally lazy, so he took the physical action to position himself near to his fitness trainer so that his environment took into account and counteracted his natural inclinations. This is different from wanting success. This is about planning for success, and about taking the necessary procedures to increase the likelihood of achieving your dreams.

He got into a state of mind which said that if everything he personally could do had been done, the results would then take care of themselves. This is one of the true secrets of any endeavour. What is it that YOU can control? When your mental energy is directed in life to the things that you have some influence over, then the mind tends to settle down and allows you to get on with the job at hand. So many people are crippled by anxiety because they are focused on the outcome as opposed to the process.

John also has a refreshing perspective on his sport. It is NOT the be-all and end-all of his persona. If the only thing in our lives is basketball then we are in a fragile emotional position. The rounded life of the developed personality is, in my opinion, one of the most important area for coaches to work on. We all must value ourselves more than what our results in a given area tell us.

Whether in business or in sport, we all need a balance and a perspective to our lives that John clearly identifies. It would be a lucky person who gets to work with him now in his role as a psychologist. How could you not be helped by a man who has been so successful, but has had the intelligence to strip apart the component parts of what it takes to be the best?

GEOFFREY BOYCOTT, OBE

Geoffrey Boycott OBE was born on 21st October 1940 in Fitzwilliam, Yorkshire. He is a former cricketer for Yorkshire and England. He was educated at Fitzwilliam Primary School, Kingsley Secondary Modern School and Hemsworth Grammar School in Yorkshire. Aged 21, Boycott made his county debut and in the following year, his first full season, he came second in the national batting averages, scoring 1,446 runs at an average of 46.64.

He made his Test debut against Australia on 4th June 1964 and in 108 test matches, Boycott scored 8,114 runs at an average of 47.72, placing him fourth on England's all-time list of run-scorers. He scored 22 centuries for his country (a joint record) and whenever he did so, England did not lose. Since retiring as a player, Boycott has found further success as a cricket commentator and writer.

QUESTIONS

What's your very first memory of cricket?

My very first memory is of playing in the street. I grew up in a two-up, two-down, back-to-back house, just like Coronation Street. We always used to play in the street – everyone used to in those days. Cricket was the summer game, soccer or rugby the winter game. The great thing about terraced houses and the coalmining community (my father was a coal miner) was that it was very safe because your parents knew where you were. Playing cricket in the street with other kids, we used a manhole cover as the wickets. There were always disputes about whether the ball had hit the top of the stumps or whether it was too high, but that was the fun of it. If you hit it in Mrs So-and-So's garden, then you were out, because we would never get the ball back. You had to go and get it before she came out and gave you a right telling-off. You had to go and get it quickly or else the game was over. It was one ball and one bat, so that was it. They were fun times. I wouldn't have swapped it. I know it was basic, but it was fun!

Who introduced you to cricket and when did you first play the game?

It was 1951, Festival of Britain year. There was a national competition which had started for primary schools that year. You played in your area against teams in 20-over cricket. Today they talk about 20-over cricket as if it is some fantastic new thing. We were playing it at school 60 years ago! This was a knock-out competition. We were pretty good. The great thing about it was that it was competitive. There were teachers who stayed behind after school to practise with you, to coach you. I can still remember my teachers, Mr Andrews and Mr Weaver. They were such an important part of my life and my development. All of the results were printed in one of the newspapers. The winners of the best performances for batting, bowling and all-rounder each received a Len Hutton Gradidge cricket bat and, because in one game I hit 45 not out when we knocked off 53 to win, as well as taking six wickets for ten runs, I won the all-rounder's prize. I was presented with this Gradidge bat – it was pure white with black letters on - and this was on the stage at school. It was a magical moment for me as a kid.

You had a bad accident as a child. What happened?

I fell over some railings when I was 10 onto the old wheel of a wringer machine, an old-fashioned washing implement. There were no washing machines in those days. The washing was boiled in a copper with a fire underneath and the surplus water was squeezed out by a wringer. I fell over the railings onto the wringer and landed on my chest and I ruptured my spleen. I was pretty poorly as it had been bleeding all night internally and it would have killed me, but for the luck of my grandmother coming to the house. She had come to see my Mum and me because she'd heard that I wasn't well. My Dad had come off the night shift and she pressured my Dad into going to get the doctor. As we didn't have a phone, he had to pedal on his bike. The doctor came and sent for the ambulance and, at the hospital, I had an emergency operation. If it hadn't been for my grandmother's persistence and my father's pedalling, I'd have been dead in another few hours.

You worked as a clerk at the Ministry of Pensions and National Insurance in Barnsley before you got a county contract. Looking back, do you think this job helped you to become a professional cricketer?

I think in the past it was harder for players to become a county cricketer. We weren't protected. Today at Yorkshire, they are taking kids on when they leave school and are paying them a salary. They practise and train and they have all kinds of coaches to help them. We didn't have any of that; we had to have other jobs to support ourselves. Today's players can dedicate 100% of their time to cricket, and this is good as it advances them as cricketers, but it also mollycoddles them a bit. I don't know that I would necessarily choose to have it that way now, but having a job made you much more independent and much more determined. For the last 15 years or so, players have had it too easy. There are so many people there to help them, they don't have to think for themselves. I had to work and also still try to have the ambition to play cricket. You had to join a club, take your own equipment to practice and get yourself back home – and organise your own tea in between. It was hard, but I think it was good for me, as it actually made me stronger and mentally tougher - I had to think for myself and do a lot more for myself. It's an easier way of life today and there's a lot more financial reward. I'm not sure it necessarily makes them better players and I am not sure that it helps to develop their character either.

At what point did you think that you would be able to play cricket for a living and turn your hobby into a full-time profession?

It was probably during my second year as a capped player for Yorkshire. Even though I was playing in the first team in 1963, I still had no contract. I just got the match fees. By then, I had decided to give up my job at the Civil Service, so I was depending on getting picked to get my match fee. It was only after the end of that season, when I got my cap in September, that they gave me a contract. That year, despite only being beaten in the national batting averages by Ken Barrington, I didn't get picked to go on England's winter tour to India. Now you work that out! It was after 1964, when I played for England and had a great season for Yorkshire, that I thought I might have a career in cricket.

Who was the biggest single influence in helping you get there?

Two people: my uncle Algy Speight, and Johnny Lawrence. Uncle Algy played in the local leagues at Ackworth and he gave me advice and took me down to the cricket field. I used to carry his bag to the matches. I learnt how to score, putting the old tins on the scoreboard. He encouraged me to move clubs from Ackworth to Barnsley, to a bigger club, not necessarily better, but bigger. Barnsley played in a higher league and the second team at Barnsley was equal to Ackworth's first team. I was 15 at the time and still at grammar school but very quickly the Vice-President at Barnsley, Clifford Hesketh, got me to the coaching at Yorkshire nets and to Johnny Lawrence's Indoor Cricket School. Johnny Lawrence was a Yorkshireman who bowled leg-spinners and batted for Somerset. Johnny was the second biggest influence, as I went to him for advice all through my cricketing life. When I was a kid, I went every Saturday morning in the winter – I had to catch two buses and walk about three quarters of a mile – and it was the best time of my life. Rain, snow, frost, it didn't matter. It was always freezing cold, but I'd always be there. Even when I played for England years later, I used to go to Johnny and practise with him weeks before I went on tour. He knew my game inside out and he was fantastic. He was like everybody's favourite grandfather. He was like Father Christmas every day you met him, full of genial life, good humour and encouragement. But he was incredibly knowledgeable too.

What was the big breakthrough moment in your career?

It was the Roses match at Bramhall Lane, Sheffield in 1963. In those days, the Roses match (between Yorkshire and Lancashire) was a huge event, with crowds of 15,000 or more, so it felt just like a Test match. We bowled Lancashire out on the Saturday and we had to bat that evening. I was due to bat at number 6 or 7, behind Raymond Illingworth, who was a very good player. So I went to the nets and I had a couple of the guys bowl to me, including the 12th man, Mel Ryan, and I got a message to go quickly. I had to pad up as we'd lost three very quick wickets. I went in as nightwatchman and I think I was 19 not out at the end of the day's play. We had the Sunday off and on the Monday, a blazing hot day, I made 145 in front of a full house, against an attack which included Brian Statham, the great England fast bowler. That innings was the big breakthrough for me; to make a big hundred in a Roses match. And we won the match too!

What sacrifices have you had to make in order to achieve success?

I wouldn't say I have sacrificed anything. I just wanted to play cricket. It was never a sacrifice for me to go and practise several times a week. Unlike most kids growing up into their late teens, early 20's, I never drank, so again that was not a sacrifice. To this day, I have never had a glass of beer. At that age, if I had been given a choice between taking a girl out or batting in the nets, it would have been batting every time. I'm very fond of ladies but I would sooner bat, every time. When people talk of sacrifice, what else is there? Batting was my love; I still love it today. I still love watching cricket. I had that will, that desire, to play cricket whenever possible.

If there was one piece of advice that helped you become successful, what was it?

My Uncle Algy once said to me *"Stay in. It's better those other buggers watch you bat than you in the pavilion watching them bat."* That was the best advice I ever had.

Did you have a set routine for mentally preparing before each innings?

Oh, yes. It wasn't rocket science; I think any kid could follow it. If you want to succeed at something, just to turn up and hope it will be alright on the day, is bloody stupid! I can't think of any other word for it. If you really care about something and want to be successful, then give it a bit of thought, put a little bit into it. Just take time to sit down for ten minutes to think about the opposition, the type of pitch you are going to play on, because those 22 yards are vital, absolutely priceless. It's still important today, but it was even more important in my day when we played on uncovered pitches, as there was no way of knowing what you were going to get from one day to the next. So, you must give a bit of thought as to what sort of surface it is and how you are going to play the opposition bowlers, which shots are safe and which shots are dodgy. Doing this is vitally important because if you make one mistake as a batsman, you have had it.

How did you practise to recreate real game-scenarios?

I believe what Jack Nicklaus once said. If you come to a big tournament and you need to practise something that you are not good at or try to improve on something, then it's a bit late. You need to be doing that weeks and months beforehand. By the time you get to the tournament or the cricket match, you should be bringing your 'A' game. I used practice in different ways. If it wasn't a match day, I would be practising particular shots. If it was match day and I was playing well, I might not stay in the nets very long. I'd always make sure my feet were moving. Batting is all about footwork; if you get the footwork wrong, then the balance isn't good. It's like a dancer, it's all about their footwork and balance. If anything is out of sync, then you are knackered. And I believe that is the key to batting; it's what Sir Donald Bradman said and I have read about it since. So I would work on that as much as anything and if I was in good form, I could see no point in batting for ages in the nets before a match. I would just do enough to feel good. Of course if I was not playing very well, I would practise a bit more, trying to get rhythm, trying to get the feel of the feet moving where I wanted them to go.

How difficult is it captaining a cricket team?

I think it is pretty difficult because, firstly, you need to have special qualities in handling people, having ten other people in the side. Secondly, you need to make time for your own game. You are a part of the team and you can't just turn up and do nothing, especially in the modern era. You really need to contribute, otherwise you are effectively playing with ten men. Thirdly, there's the tactical side of the game. The two important facets that a captain should have are tactical ability and the ability to handle people. It's hard enough finding the people who have one of these facets. Finding someone to do both, wow! But every team needs a captain. Of course it helps if you have a good team. You need ten other individuals who are good.

Did you enjoy captaincy or not?

I loved the tactical side of the job. I wasn't especially good at dealing with people but I was brilliant tactically. I can see things very quickly and that's why I understand the game and can talk about it when I am commentating. Some people don't see things as I do. I actually don't believe you grow into captaincy. I think you either have it or you don't. It's a gift to be able to see things happen before they happen; the great captains are two steps ahead of the game. They don't wait for it to happen and they don't just follow the ball. And believe me, there aren't many good ones around and there haven't been many in the history of the game. There has only been a handful who have been superb at it, because it's bloody difficult.

How would you help someone who wasn't as mentally tough as yourself?

I don't think you can. If people ask me for advice, I give it. Some people of course don't want to be given advice. If it was in the dressing room and we were talking about winning the match, that was different and I'd say what I would think about how we could do better. In a team sport like cricket, you are constantly talking about tactics – at lunchtime, tea, end of play, start of play. As a captain, if you don't have a discussion with other players, then you're an idiot, especially with your senior players. It's no different from people in all walks of life. If a commander in the armed forces thinks he can just do it on his own, he's going to make some serious mistakes. He needs to have two or three people with whom he can talk before he can make a decision - not by consensus, not by a show of hands, but his.

Do you think you can control your mind?

When I was batting, yes. That was the one place I knew I could control things. It was different away from the crease. I'm two people. On the field, when I was batting, I could control myself and my emotions. I could count the number of balls gone in an over, those to come. I counted every run I got. In one-day matches, where there were five or six bowlers, I could keep in my head how many overs they had each bowled and how many they had to come, which was useful as it allowed me to calculate which bowlers to go after and which to defend against. I think all that is part of having a good cricket mind – to carry all these things in your head and still be able to concentrate on the ball, one ball at a time as it comes down.

Did you have periods in your career where you doubted yourself?

I never doubted myself, but I did lose confidence and conviction whenever I had a run of bad form. It's harder to get out of form today because they play on better pitches. It's not impossible, but it's harder. In our day, it was much easier to get out of form because you had some summers which were very wet and the covering was quite poor. Today there are hydrofoils and they are fantastic. In our day, you had a bit of plastic on wheels about eight inches above the surface. Rain doesn't come straight down, it sheets at an angle, so the wind used to blow the rain underneath the covers. It was much easier to have periods of poor form. Not just for my generation, but for players before me too – even all the greats. I have read quite a lot about them, and very few could maintain their career without having some period of difficulty.

What did you do when you felt nervous?

I was always nervous. I think it is vital to have nerves. Anybody who isn't nervous is either a liar or an idiot. The key to having nerves is to channel them into positive energy. If you are not nervous, I think it's because you don't care. You're only nervous because you *do* care about it. It doesn't matter whether you are going for a job interview or you're batting for England, you care. You are nervous because you don't want to fail and embarrass yourself, you want to do well. It therefore heightens your senses. If you're good, you channel that into positive energy, not negative.

What game would you single out as being the most nervous you have ever been?

It was my comeback game for England at Nottingham against Australia in 1977. I hadn't played Test cricket for three years. A lot of people wanted me to come back and succeed, but there were some that didn't, so it was a very stressful time. We were playing a pretty good side on quite a bouncy pitch. Len Pascoe and Jeff Thomson were bowling, and they could play. I was 36 at the time, which is an age when people are normally retired. So I needed to show mental strength and character. I knew I was going to get a lot of short deliveries as the Aussie bowlers would always test my courage and my technique. They were thinking: is he past it? will he bottle it? I didn't. I got a 107 and 80 not out and we won the match.

When you were under extreme pressure, how did you deal with that?

I would always say, deal with it - be glad of it. Don't try and suppress it at all. Don't pretend it's not there. Being nervous and feeling under pressure are normal human traits. If you hear people are nerveless, it's codswallop.

What is the best example of you being at your very best?

It would be during the 1970-71 tour of Australia - when we won the Ashes under Raymond Illingworth – and then the following summer in England. My record on that Ashes tour was exceptionally good, although I had my arm broken by Graham McKenzie just before the end of the last Test in Sydney, which meant I was out for three months. When I came back, I averaged 100 on uncovered pitches. Today, they play on flat pitches like the Oval. I could bat on them with a stick of rhubarb!

How have you dealt with personal criticism over the years?

It's not easy sometimes. It's something you have to try to deal with because you are in the public eye. If it's fair, then it's easier to accept. But how often is it fair? We live in a democracy and I believe in free speech, so you just have to accept it. The one thing which I really don't like is when people write articles about you, or speak about you, and the only way they know you is through reading lots of cuttings. They haven't met me personally, probably have never even seen me bat. I see articles written today by younger people, who never saw me bat because I haven't played for over 20 years. They will read things written by other people – which are very often untrue. And then, to get these comments put right, you have a huge legal process to go through, costing money and time. Who has the money and who has the time? It's unfair when they repeat things that are untrue.

What's been the most important ingredient in your achieving success?

Desire. I would ask any young kid, how much do you want it? How badly do you want to play cricket?

Would you do anything differently if you had your time again?

I hope so, otherwise I have learnt nothing. I would say that to everybody. Anyone who says they would do the same again, I can never understand. It means they have learnt nothing. We should all learn from the experiences and mistakes we have made in life - and I have made plenty - and if I had the time again, I'd try to do things better.

Success seems to have been very important to you. What fuelled this desire in you to be successful?

I'm not sure it has been special to me. But I'm also not sure why anyone would want to play and only be moderate or average. I can't see any point in that. My view is to let the others be moderate and average. I always wanted to be the best I could be.

In 2002 you were diagnosed as having throat cancer. How difficult was the laser treatment and how strong did you have to be to recover from it?

In all, I had 35 sessions of laser and it burns your whole skin, your neck, your chest. It's pretty gruelling and unpleasant. You have to be strong, mentally strong, when the doctors are treating you for cancer – and they are doing everything they can for many people today. But they can never guarantee it will be successful. Every cancer-patient will know that's the one thing that can affect your mind. Even though you go through terrific difficulties, you are not sure if it is going to work.

What one-line sentence would you give to anybody aspiring to be the best they could be?

If you want it badly enough, keep going. Don't let anyone talk you out of it.

Which sportsman or woman do you admire the most and why?

From the cricket world, Douglas Jardine. He found a way to cut down the greatest batsman cricket has ever seen – Donald Bradman - to cut him down to 50% of what he was averaging. Jardine knew that you couldn't beat Australia with Bradman averaging 100 every innings. He needed to get him out. So, he worked out the 'bodyline' strategy which was well within the rules and he was clever enough, and ruthless enough, to carry it out. And almost every member of the team with him spoke highly of him. Only Gubby Allen, and the manager Plum Warner, were against it. Although he got criticism from other people of that era, and the Australians who were badly beaten, there were people like Harold Larwood and Herbert Sutcliffe who spoke warmly and highly of him. Jardine was clever and ruthless. What a figure he must have been to have carried everyone in the team with him through that time - all apart from two.

Outside of cricket, the one I laugh most about is Cassius Clay (Muhammad Ali) - brilliant, absolutely fantastic. He made you laugh, he was absolutely unbelievable. Funny, talented, a winner – he had everything.

Also, probably the best footballer I've ever seen, George Best - he was a genius.

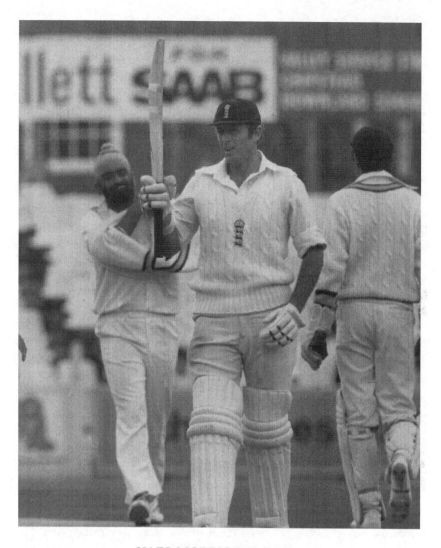

KARL MORRIS SUMMARY

As ever, Geoffrey Boycott is totally forthright in his views and opinions of what it takes to become the very best you can be. You cannot help but admire a man who by sheer guts and determination became one of the finest cricketers England has ever produced. In a similar way to Kevin Keegan in football and Padraig Harrington in golf, he was perhaps not the most naturally gifted player, but Boycott became a run-machine through applying himself systematically to his craft.

It is fascinating that Geoffrey makes the comment the only time he felt totally 'in control' was when he was out in the middle batting. This brings to light one of the most important ingredients to success, 'perceived control'. When we feel that we are in control of a situation, the mind tends to calm down and we get on with the job in hand. This is why people are irrationally scared of flying as opposed to driving because they feel they have no control of the situation.

It is clear Geoffrey focused on the things that HE could control when he was at the crease. He 'knew' the bowlers, he had prepared in his mind beforehand for the state of the pitch, he had a plan which bowlers to attack and which to play cautiously. He was absorbed in what HE could do in the given situation. This, I would go as far as to say, is one of the 'secrets' of life, let alone cricket - focus on what YOU can control in any given situation, what you can have some influence over.

So many people wreck their lives because they focus almost entirely on things that they have little or no control over: other people, economies, the weather - the list is a long one: these are things we really should not give our mental energy to. I have a simple equation: life is just TWO columns or lists. Column one is about the things I can control and column two is about the things I can't control. Success is about being in column one MOST of the time and recognising when you have slipped into column two and getting yourself back on track.

Geoffrey Boycott clearly spent most of his time in column one. He found his purpose in life out in the middle and, as he says to this day, he still loves to watch and absorb himself in the game. This is a throwback to a time when people played sport for the sheer joy of the game they loved, as opposed to any possible material gain. This is the very antithesis of what I call our 'X-Factor' generation, wanting to 'be famous'. Nobody should really want to be famous. We should all strive to be absorbed, fascinated and passionate about something which strikes a chord deep within us. If we do, then fame and money may well be around the corner, but above anything else, we will be doing the thing we love.

LAURA DAVIES, CBE

Laura Jane Davies CBE was born on 5th October 1963 in Coventry, England and is a professional golfer. She was educated at The Grange School and Fullbrook County Secondary School in New Haw, Surrey.

She is considered the most accomplished English female golfer of modern times, being the first non-American, to finish at the top of the LPGA money list. She has won the Ladies' European Tour Order of Merit a record seven times: in 1985, 1986, 1992, 1996, 1999, 2004 and 2006.

She currently has 74 professional wins worldwide, 20 on the LPGA tour, including four major titles. She is a member of the US-based LPGA tour and a life member of the Ladies' European Tour. She needs only one major victory or two regular tour wins to enter the LPGA Hall of Fame.

Davies also commentates for the BBC and is a mad keen sports fan.

QUESTIONS

What is your first golfing memory?

Hitting a golf ball into a blanket in the back garden at New Haw with my brother Tony. He had a set of clubs and the tradition, on our birthdays, was whatever one of us got, the other one got a little present too. On my 12th birthday, my mother and step-dad bought me a 5-iron and Tony was out in the garden hitting shots, so I took my 5-iron out there and started hitting balls into the blanket as well.

When and where did you first properly take up the game?

I was 14. My Aunt Maria and Uncle Les were members at Merrow Golf Club near Guildford. I showed some interest in the game and I used to go to the club and have a putt. And soon they got me in as a junior and I started to play a few matches for the club. When I was 16, I was good enough to be selected for England juniors, while also playing in amateur tournaments. I didn't have a particularly successful amateur career, winning a few events but nothing special. You would never have marked me out to be one of the up-and-coming young players. At that time Clare Waite was the top amateur in the world and we were playing against each other every week and she was beating me hands down. Janet Collingham (as she was then) was another one you would have earmarked for the future. I had a steady amateur career and then turned professional at the age of 21, when it all started to happen.

Did learning the game always come naturally to you?

I've always played sport. Whatever sport is there, I will have a go at it. I have a snooker table at home. I love darts too. When I practised golf with Tony my brother, I found it easy. I never played air-shots. My first handicap was 26, but then it started to tumble fairly quickly.

As a junior golfer, who were your heroes?

At that time, the best players were Seve Ballesteros, Jack Nicklaus, Bernhard Langer and Ian Woosnam. They were the ones who were playing fantastic golf. Anyone who watches Seve wants to play golf. So that's what I started to do. I watched Seve and Bernhard Langer on television, and Mum and Mike (my step-dad) would take us over to Woburn, Wentworth or Walton Heath, all fairly close to us, whenever those players were there.

Whilst developing as an amateur golfer, how often would you play a week?

In the summer holidays, Tony and I played 54 holes a day almost every day. We'd go round three times a day, and were on the range before and after. Mum would drop us off on her way to work and would come and pick us up in the evening. If we couldn't get a lift to the club, Tony and I would go down to Heathervale Park. We weren't really allowed to play down there or hit long shots, but we used to take a few golf balls and hit them back and forth to each other. I never got bored of playing. I just wanted to get better. That's the thing about golf; you have never beaten it. I've been a professional for 23 years and have won a few tournaments, but I still want to win the next tournament I play in. Every year, I want to finish strongly and then look forward to the next year.

Who was the main person responsible for teaching you the game?

I've never had a lesson in my life. It was just Tony and me on the range. I'd try and swing like Seve. We'd watch television and just try and mimic the players. We had a couple of friends who were keen golfers, so there would usually be four of us playing. When I got into the England team, Vivien Saunders used to be the national coach, but I never had a lesson, mainly because I wasn't a very good listener. I was a natural at most sports and I didn't see why golf should be any different. It's not a reaction sport. Golf is all in the mind. Any problems I have had as a professional have been in the mind. When I was a junior, I had no problem, because you just don't think, you do it. My biggest fault is that I see bad shots instead of good shots. I am playing really well at the moment, but in the middle of the year, I was just seeing all the wrong shots. Now I just look straight down the fairway and hit it where I want to go. It's nothing technical; it's just bad thoughts that make you play badly.

Did you always have the ambition to be a professional golfer?

By the age of 16, I was playing off 8, which was when I wanted to leave school and become a professional. I never had much interest in school. I used to love going to school, but I knew I wanted to do something in sport. At the time, the Ladies' European Tour had just started up, and Nancy Lopez was big news in America and I knew that golf was what I wanted to do. It's never been an obsession. Even today, I'm always looking to get away from the golf. But in the early days, it was golf, golf, golf because you are young and it's fun. It's no different to kicking a football if you are a real football fan. I had to do work-experience and at the time I was a Truancy Officer for the area, which was up at the New Zealand Golf Club. I went to my Head of Year and said I wanted to play golf as my work experience. So, everyone else was off doing various different things and I was on the golf course.

Having made your mind up that you wanted to be a professional, how were the years between 16 and 21?

I had a winter job every year. I worked for three years at Sainsbury's in Chertsey, one year at a garage in Woking behind the till, and then I had one year at Coral's in Woking. I had these winter jobs for about seven months and then, for the five months in the summer, I'd just be playing golf in amateur events. Mum and Mike used to ferry me around, but by the time I was 18 I had my own car so I could take myself and other mates to tournaments. I was doing well at these events. I won the Welsh Open which was one of the biggest ones. From a handicap point of view, I was stuck on 8 for a while and then all of a sudden I was off scratch and by the time I turned professional, I was plus 5. So, aged 17, when I was playing proper junior events, I was down to scratch.

So you went from a 26 handicap to plus 5 without ever having had a single lesson?

Although I was a junior member at Merrow, West Byfleet Golf Club was closest to me, so I used to go down there as a junior member too and they were very good to me as I didn't have any family there. David Regan was the head professional at West Byfleet and he used to come out on the range and just watch me hit balls. I would ask him one or two things, but he would never stand there and give me advice about my grip or anything, so I have never had a set of formal lessons. Joanne Carner, on the Women's Tour, has helped me with my bunker play but I don't consider that as being lessons as such. I have basically never had a coach. I've played golf with some of the best players in the world and, if you are playing with Seve for example, you want him to show you a few chip shots. I developed a really nice flop shot watching Seve out in Japan when we were paired together in an event. So that's my coaching; I've gone to the best.

Having won various amateur tournaments in 1983 and 1984, you turned professional in 1985 and you won both the Rookie of the Year and Order of Merit titles in your debut season. That's some start to your professional career. What enabled you to hit the ground running with such effect?

I just took to the format. There is a lot of matchplay in amateur golf and I have never been brilliant at matchplay, whereas three or four rounds of strokeplay seemed to work better for me. I used to qualify well in English Amateurs and British Amateurs, as it was strokeplay to qualify but then matchplay after that. I would always qualify high and then get knocked out, so I suppose strokeplay was better for me as a professional. When I turned pro, I was 21 and wasn't scared of anything. The youngsters now seem to be a different breed – 14-year-olds who are much taller and more mature-looking – whereas, when I started, most of the people my age were turning professional at 21.

You won your first major, the US Women's Open, in 1987. Was this your big breakthrough moment?

It was because I won in America. I'd probably won five or six times on the European Tour before that, but to go to America was something different. We all went out there - myself, my brother, my cousin

Matthew and my Dad who lived in America – and we just thought we were going to have a great holiday, I'd miss the cut and we'd come home. But at the end, three of us were tied at the finish of the fourth round, so I was playing off against Ayako Imoto from Japan and Joanne Carner who was the big legend of American golf and a great lady and fantastic fun. I don't remember the actual scoring but I was always there or thereabouts. On the 17th, I had a two-shot lead on a par 5 – and I went for it in two. Joanne looked across at me and she couldn't believe that I had gone for it as she thought I should have been laying up. I birdied that hole and made a putt on 18 to win by 2 shots. That was the only time I thought, "Bloody hell, I have won the Open." I'll never forget Joanne looking over at me just shaking her head. I think she thought it was a bit reckless going for it on this particular occasion, but that is what you do if you are fearless.

It must have been a great feeling to have won it and to have reached such a significant landmark?

It was but we had to get on a plane almost immediately to get back for the Women's British Open at St Mellion. It was all a bit of a whirlwind, but I finished second to Alison Nicholas. So it was nearly two majors in six days which would have been nice. I remember a couple of people at the airport when we landed taking pictures of me which was very foreign to me. All of a sudden though, things had changed. I was on *A Question of Sport*, which was my favourite television programme, and there was lots of other stuff like that which started happening which was nice.

How do you approach a tournament? Do you take it shot by shot and hole by hole or, before each round, do you set yourself a target?

You know how hard the course is, so, in your mind, you therefore have a rough idea of what the winning score will be and you then try to reach that winning score after four rounds. You always want to shoot 8 under on the first day, but you'll take 2 under. Golf is not a sprint; it's about not doing too much damage over the first three days, and trying to be in contention on the Sunday. When you are playing well, you don't think about anything other than the next shot you face. When you are playing badly, you might think about the next tee-shot you don't like. When you are playing well, it's automatic - you cruise along and nothing gets in your way.

In your career then, how often would you say you were playing well and how often would you have some mental demons?

For five years I was the number-one player in the world. And for three of those years I was on auto-pilot. I won 24 tournaments in three seasons and it all seemed so easy. Even in the ones where I didn't win, I was second, third or at least somewhere in the top ten just like Annika Sörenstam used to do and now Lorena Ochoa. Nowadays, it is not so easy because I think too much about it and that's what gets in your way. Between 1994 and 1996, it was about as easy as it could get. Everyone who gets to that level feels that. They must do. I'm no different to anyone else. It just came ridiculously easy, but now I know it's not!

What gives you the most pleasure: a fantastic drive, a great shot onto the green, a brilliant chip out of the bunker or a superb putt?

The most exciting thing is to make a superb putt, because you get the reaction from the gallery. The most satisfying, though, is a long iron into a tight pin. I hit one recently in Houston. The other girls didn't take it on, but I had it to within 10 feet, but missed the putt so that ruined it!

Can you talk me through your pre-shot routine?

My caddy, Johnny Scott, and I stand at the bag. Johnny gives me the number; we talk about the club. I never have a practice-swing. I pick my point, the club goes down behind the ball, I then take a couple of looks at the flag. If it's an iron onto the green, my tee-shots are slightly different. Hopefully, you don't think about the swing, because that's when you struggle. If you just put your club down, get your point, swing, and the ball goes where you intend it to, then you know you are playing well. I pick a line by looking at the flag, then draw a line down about a foot in front of the ball, I then put the club head down on that line so I know the club head is square. Then, if I fade it, I open my stance, but normally I am trying to hit it dead straight with a little fall out left to right. That's it, you should be lined up and ready to go.

When you're having a bad round, how do you go about steadying the ship?

I'll ask Johnny whether I am swinging too quickly or not. Whether I am or not, we always concentrate on slowing the swing down. If I get it wrong, it's because I have seen a bad shot in my mind, and I go a bit quick. Johnny says he can tell by the way I stand over the ball if I am going to hit a good one or a bad one. I've worked with Johnny for nearly four years now and he can spot the signs. He knows if I am over the ball with a nice two or three waggles and a smooth takeaway, he's 99% confident it will go dead straight. If I move a bit quicker, he knows I have problem with the shot. It doesn't always turn out to be a bad one, but there is more chance of it being a bad one.

How important is the relationship between golfer and caddy?

I think it is the most important thing there is. All the really good players have their caddies for a long time. It surprises me how the slightly less good players have not twigged onto that. They chop and change and I don't think they understand. They think their part in it is so important that the caddy is irrelevant. That's certainly the impression I get.

How difficult is it for caddies to trust themselves to speak up and say something at an important moment?

That's the difference between a good caddy and a bad caddy. The good caddy will say stuff and the bad caddy will stand back and just be a yes-man. On tour, the yes-men are the worst caddies. Simple as that. I listen to my caddy every time. If he is wrong more than he is right and he ends up being rubbish, then you get rid of him. In 23 years of playing, I have had six regular caddies. They are all decent golfers and know when they need to step in. Johnny never steps in if I am getting a bit quick, because it is not every time and he knows I hate backing off from a shot. Once I am over the ball, he knows I want to hit. It has to be an extreme case for him to call me off the ball. It would never be because he thinks I am going to hit a bad shot, it would be because of a gust of wind for instance. From a clubbing and numbers point of view, every caddy should be able to add up and every caddy should roughly know how far their player hits it. I don't go in for the lining up of putts, I think it should be outlawed, along with the long-handled putters. You get some caddies lining up a tee-shot, lining up an iron-shot and then lining up a putt, and one of the greatest parts of golf is alignment. And then you have someone there saying do this, do that which I think is ludicrous.

Do you have a set routine for mentally preparing before each round?

We turn up at the course about an hour before the tee-off time. We go to the range, the putting green, the chipping green and then away. If I am in contention on a Sunday, I might be a little quieter, maybe a little more liable to snap if Johnny says something I don't like. He knows when I really have a chance to win, because I get a little more into it than I normally would be.

Do you think you can control your mind?

I wish I could. That's my biggest problem. I'm probably still the best ball-striker in the women's game, but I'm just not the best mentally out there on the course. I've been doing it for so long, but when you are younger, it's easier to forget about the bad shots. Now I always feel as if I am trying to prove myself. People ask me when I am going to retire and remind me that I am 46. Then you think, "Sod that, I can still win," and I do. I haven't won in America for the last seven seasons, but I have won every year in Europe. I just want to prove that I can still do it to shut the people up who question why I am still playing. If I could control that, and just blank it all out, it would be very good.

What do you feel is your most destructive emotion and how do you deal with it?

Shaun, a friend's husband, who caddied for me for a while, said I should just concentrate on the back of the ball whenever I address the ball. Before, on the tee, for a nervy shot, I'd be looking here, there and everywhere. I don't know what emotion you would call that, but it has been a real issue for me. In the Solheim Cup once in the singles on the Sunday, I hit a horrendous tee-shot when I was two up with two to play. I was only hitting a 3-iron off the tee and Shaun was watching me in the crowd. He said he could see that, following that shot, my attitude completely changed as I was cruising at the time. A couple of weeks later, he told me to concentrate on hitting the back of the ball, don't think of anything ahead of that, and since then I have really turned the corner.

How do you deal with doubt?

It all connects to the same thing – you are worried that you are not going to hit it where you want to. With every shot, you just have to think about where you want the ball to go. You can never think about where you don't want it to go. Doubt is the thing that I have had to work against the most. When you are playing well, you simply don't think about anything. You think about what you might say in the speech afterwards. I've been in that situation three-quarters of the way through a tournament, as it all came just so easy, whereas now, it doesn't.

What do you do when you feel nervous?

I walk around. I lost a play-off in Italy a few weeks ago and I had my second shot in regulation to 18, and I just couldn't stand still. Johnny was giving me the number, but the group in front were taking forever. I just walk around when I am nervous. You can't play unless you get nervous. Even when I was winning week-in, week-out, I was still nervous. You still feel the excitement. I view nerves as a very positive thing.

What's been the hardest putt of your career – the one where you were under the most pressure?

At Nabisco in 1994, when I three-putted the 18th, having had a one-shot lead, and Donna Andrews won it. She birdied the hole, I bogeyed it and lost by a shot. She had a six-foot birdie putt and I had a 15-foot par putt. I missed that putt, and it was the most pressure I have ever felt on a putt. Had I two-putted and had she holed, it would have been a play-off, but the chances are that if I had holed mine, she would have missed hers because she had a difficult putt. The 15-footer was the result of a very bad first putt. If I could take any putt again, I really wish it could be that one. I hit it too hard and that was it. The second putt was dreadful – I pulled it.

You've played in all eleven Solheim Cups to date, the only player from Europe or the USA to have done so. What do you like most about competing in this event?

Contrary to what I said before, it is the matchplay I like. It's fun! You play foursomes and fourballs - which you don't usually do - the galleries are always full, the excitement-levels are always high and you've got the team-room. I think there's nothing better than the Solheim Cup. Having said that, I hated the last one because Allie (Alison Nicholas, Team Europe's captain) never played me. She just kept leaving me out. I had only missed two series in the whole of the first ten Solheim Cups. She sat me out for three series in one Solheim Cup which was extraordinary. Let's just say I was slightly miffed about it.

How would you describe the differences in the women's game now compared to when you first broke onto the scene?

It's the age-levels I think. When I turned professional, and particularly when I went out to America, all the best players - the Patty Sheehans, the Betsy Kings were all around 30. Now, the best players seem to be 24 or 25.

Looking back, when were you at your peak as a player?

In 1996, when I was 33. It was my best year. I won two majors, ten tournaments, I won the Skins Game, I won everything really apart from the Sports Personality of the Year, which Damon Hill won.

If there was one piece of advice that helped you become successful, what was it?

Dave Regan, the professional at West Byfleet, always told me not to have a lesson. He said he could see I was a natural, so he encouraged me to take tips from people, to listen to what you want to listen to but never get stuck in with a coach, because it might be the undoing of me. Dave was a decent pro – he used to qualify for the British Open every year - but he was more of a teaching pro. Dave gave me the confidence just to do my own thing. In those days, David Leadbetter was pulling Nick Faldo's swing to pieces, and I think he would have won more tournaments without all that nonsense.

What's been the most important ingredient in your achieving success?

The fact that I am never scared of losing. I go for every shot. Within reason, of course, as you can't be gung ho on every single shot. Never be scared to fail. That's the secret. If you have a drive over water, off the deck, onto an island green, don't lay up. You know you can hit the shot, do it, don't be scared to fail. I have failed on many an occasion. In Japan once, I was tied for third at the 18th and I hit a 3-wood and ended up in 50th place, having made an 11 at that last. I was trying to win it. I was very angry and upset, and it was awful, but at the end of the day, the next time I find myself in that position, I will probably hit a great shot and win the tournament. So, never be scared to fail.

Which sportsman or woman do you admire the most and why?

I'm a Liverpool fan and I'm a bit biased, but it has to be Steven Gerrard. I just love watching him play. He's in a different class to everybody else. Whenever I go to see Liverpool play live, and you see Steven playing at his best, I don't care what they say about any other player in the world. He is the best. He works so hard. Even though he is the best, he never makes it look like he knows he is the best as he is always encouraging the other players, slapping them on the back. That's his best quality. He tries to bring everyone up to his level, not that they could ever reach it.

From the world of golf, my two favourites are Nancy Lopez and Seve Ballesteros. It would be hard to split either of them. Nancy taught me how to be a good loser. In the early days, she was at the absolute pinnacle of the game, whereas I was just an up-and-coming player. She was so nice to me. Any time we had tournaments against each other, win or lose, she was always just a brilliant winner and a brilliant loser, and I learnt that from her. And I admire Seve for his complete attitude towards the game and his love of it.

KARL MORRIS SUMMARY

I think it was the great Scottish pro Tommy Armour who said 'you have to know golf in all of its complexity to TEACH it in all of its SIMPLICITY.' Even though Laura Davies hasn't used a coach throughout her career, I think that she would echo these very wise words. Time and time again, I have seen a player's game ruined by being over-coached. Having the mind full of HOW to do something when you are trying to DO something is not a recipe for success.

It is clear that throughout Laura's career she has kept away from this scenario and remained one of the pre-eminent forces in women's golf by trusting HER swing as opposed to looking for THE swing.

It is a refreshing message in this present world of coaching complexity and a theme that seems to run through the pages of this book. I would counter this ever so slightly, in the sense that, for some people, good technical coaching at the right time can be a massive boost to a career. The key is to have balance in this.

Know yourself and know your own technique. Seek out quality coaching if that suits you but NEVER become dependent on it. The key in sport is that when it is performed well it is due to an ABSENCE of thought as opposed to over-analysis.

It is fascinating how Laura talks about a particular method of 'quietening' her mind under pressure by just focusing on the back of the ball as opposed to letting her eyes dart all over the place.

It is no coincidence to me that she has found this tool to be effective. When the eyes are busy, the mind is busy and this tends to exaggerate feelings of tension and anxiety. Thoughts flashing across the screen of your mind, random and often disturbing, can be a sure-fire way for your performance to suffer. By calming the eyes, we CAN calm the mind. Of all of the things that you COULD focus on, you decide to focus on ONE place. This is for me the same benefit which is derived from meditation when the mind is given a focus-point or mantra to hold our attention. To train yourself to do this in pressure situations can be VERY effective.

I do love the fact that Laura still talks about the game with such passion. Even after all the time she has spent at the top, she still wants to win, still wants to prove herself and quieten the voices of doubt which inevitably rise to the surface, as a player heads towards the autumn days of a career. Again, a common thread that is shared by the rest of the superstars within these pages, she still clearly LOVES to play her sport.

Laura concludes by saying 'never be scared to fail'. I would go as far as to say that we HAVE to fail to be successful. Going for a shot on the eighteenth hole, failing spectacularly by taking an 11 and tumbling down the leaderboard is very tough to take. This is what mental toughness is about: being able to fail but then moving on and letting that 'failure' go. It is an essential quality to develop and Laura Davies has it in bundles.

SIR RANULPH FIENNES, OBE

Sir Ranulph Twisleton-Wykeham-Fiennes 3rd Baronet OBE was born on 7th March 1944 in Windsor, Berkshire. He was educated at Eton College. He is better known as Ranulph (Ran) Fiennes and is a British expedition leader and holder of several endurance records.

Fiennes served in the British army for eight years, including a period on counter-insurgency service while attached to the army of the Sultanate of Oman. He then undertook numerous expeditions, including being the first man to visit both the North and South poles by surface means and the first man completely to cross Antarctica on foot. In 2003, just four months after having suffered a heart attack and undergone a double heart-bypass operation, he completed the incredible feat of running seven marathons in seven days on seven continents. In May 2009, aged 65, he climbed to the summit of Mount Everest, becoming the oldest British person to achieve this. According to the Guinness Book of World Records, he is the world's greatest living adventurer.

QUESTIONS

You were born shortly after your father died in action in the Second World War. Growing up, he must have been a hero to you?

My father is the person I most respected from when I was a child right up till now. I never met him as he was killed in the War a few months before I was born. But my mother, and later old Army colleagues of his, told me about him.

You served in your father's regiment, the Royal Scots Greys. Was this your first major goal in life, to follow in the footsteps of your father?

Since my childhood, I always wanted to be the colonel of the Royal Scots Greys regiment which is what my father was in the War.

After eight years service, you left the military. What disillusioned you about Army life?

Nothing disillusioned me about Army life. I loved it. But I failed to get into Sandhurst due to lack of A-Levels. So I couldn't get a regular commission. That meant I could only get a maximum of eight years in the Army. I served the full eight years and then had to leave.

Who or what inspired you to want to become an adventurer?

I am not an adventurer! My passport has always stated 'Travel Writer'. I am an expedition-leader and have been since leaving the Army in 1970. I make a living out of lecturing and writing about expeditions. On leaving the Army, I had no income and had got married, so I decided to use my experience in the Army of leading soldiers on 'adventure-training exercises' (canoeing, climbing, skiing in Europe etc.) to do similar activities as a civilian, commercial business.

Is an adventurer fearless or have there been times when you have been genuinely scared?

Myself and the people on the expeditions are totally normal types who have standard 'fears' and try to avoid 'scary' situations when planning the expeditions.

Do you think fear is a good thing?

Psychologists might recommend that a bit of fear spices up an otherwise boring existence but I fail to see that logic. Fear can cause stress which in turn can cause illness.

Are you always super-confident in any challenge you undertake? Indeed, is this a pre-requisite of being an expedition leader?

When planning an expedition, I often go for 'firsts' - for example, journeys that have never previously been achieved. So I know there will be a big chance of failure. But I am confident that by planning, with attention to small details, I will stand a reasonable chance of success.

When a challenge or expedition fails for whatever reason, how quickly can you move on from the disappointment or does it rankle with you for a long time?

Whenever I fail to achieve a challenge, I don't waste any time crying over spilled milk. I start planning to try it again using the previous failure as a lesson to change tactics. My first two attempts on Everest failed, which helped me get there on the third attempt.

With the benefit of hindsight, how many of your achievements would you not have started had you known how difficult they were going to be?

The only challenge that turned out to be so unpleasant that, if I'd had the ability to see into the future I would not have tried it, was the climbing of the North Face of the Eiger in 2007. I made it to the top but really disliked most of the climb.

Which do you enjoy more - a solo challenge or one with team-mates?

Journeys done alone can be very boring. Also, much of the fun of expeditions is the planning of them with colleagues and later the memories to recall with the folk who were there with you.

Do you think you can control your mind?

I would have failed many of my past challenges if I had not been able to shut down pessimistic or weak thoughts interfering with my mind. I often lose this 'thoughts-battle' but not always.

When you are under extreme pressure, how do you deal with that?

When under pressure, I become ponderous. I need to focus and put one foot forward really slowly before taking the next step to escape from the pressure-situation.

What is the best example of you being at your very best?

I set group and personal targets, such as how many miles to progress in a day of difficult or dangerous travel. If, at the end of a really nasty day, we've stuck to the schedule through all the problems, then that's the best of times.

What do you dislike about your sport?

When the route of a challenge involves huge drops down (as on the Eiger climb). I dislike that intensely.

What's been the most important ingredient in your achieving success?

Luck. This can come in the form of good weather coinciding with really tricky ice-conditions or simply passing over a hidden crevasse a few inches to the left or the right of a fracture.

What would you do differently if you had your time again?

I would try harder.

What one-line sentence would you give to anybody aspiring to be the best they could be?

You need to know when to give up and never do so a second earlier than you need.

Which sportsman or sportswoman from another sport do you admire the most and why?

I admire Steve Redgrave and Paula Radcliffe for their long, long years of utter dedication to their sport.

KARL MORRIS SUMMARY

In these current times of economic turmoil and job-loss, I think that it is important to look at Sir Ranulph Fiennes' story and dig a little bit deeper than the obvious outstanding, adventure explorations. Due to the immense respect for his late father's legacy, first and foremost, he wanted to be in the Army. This he did and 'loved it', yet because of a lack of the required A-levels and not being able to go to Sandhurst, he was only able to stay in the army for eight years.

Having left with no income, Sir Ranulph decided to turn his existing skills of organising expeditions into a business. What an incredible story that decision has left behind for us all. Yet, maybe the more important message is that life will always be a series of transitory phases for us all. Nothing lasts forever. We all need to be aware that, as life throws these changes at us, be that in sport, business or life, we all need to be open enough and brave enough to see these transitions as opportunities, as opposed to fearing the end of an existing, known world.

Careers for life are now probably a thing of the past. Sportsmen and women face the inevitable fact that life at the top is going to be relatively short-lived. I, for one, have seen too many lives devastated by trying to cling on to past glories and not being able to replace a sense of purpose in life. The phrase "the only thing constant is change" maybe an overused cliché, but it is so particularly true. It also reinforces the fact it is so very important to celebrate the good times and experiences that we currently have; to realise the daily training, the challenges and the frustrations are actually part of a glorious period called NOW. The balance between moving on when we need to and soaking up and enjoying what we have now is a uniquely human challenge.

The most dangerous arena of our mind is perhaps the past. If we are constantly reminiscing about how good it used to be, and unfortunately many folk who lose the essential spark of life fall into this most debilitating of mental habits.

It is not a problem that Sir Ranulph has, because there is always another challenge waiting around the corner, always another metaphorical mountain to climb. It is what keeps him alive and it is what we should all seek to emulate.

ANDREW FLINTOFF, MBE

Andrew Flintoff MBE was born on 6th December 1977 in Preston, Lancashire. He was educated at Greenlands County Primary School and Ribbleton Hall High School. He is a cricketer who plays for Lancashire, England and the Indian Premier League Team Chennai Super Kings. He recently retired from Test cricket, having helped England to regain the Ashes in a 2-1 series win against Australia in 2009.

At the end of the Ashes series in 2005, he was named Player of the Series, having scored 402 runs at an average of 40.20 and taken 24 wickets at 27.29. This achievement saw him crowned BBC Sports Personality of the Year in 2005, the first time a cricketer had won it since Ian Botham in 1981.

QUESTIONS

You were probably too young to remember the Ashes series in 1981, so what was your first cricketing memory?

I have now seen quite a lot of the 1981 Ashes series on television, but my first cricketing memory was my Dad playing local Saturday afternoon cricket for Dutton Forshaw, who played at a school ground in those days.

Who introduced you to cricket and when did you first play the game?

My Dad introduced me to the game and I had my first game at the age of 6. My father has always been very passionate about the game, and we were a real cricketing family. We didn't play at school, but my Dad played on Saturday afternoons. Me and my brother Chris, who is a little older than me, used to play on the side of the pitch, before progressing to the middle. My Mum made the teas, my grandparents came to watch, my Auntie Ennis and Uncle Ted were there. It was a real family thing.

What did cricket mean to you as a child?

I loved it - from the moment I can remember it. Obviously, other sports were played at school but I only played football to be accepted. I played so I didn't get beaten up every day! Playing for Lancashire for the first time aged 9 and being involved in the county and getting my first cap meant everything to me. When I realised you could get paid for playing cricket as well, I always wanted to do it. I remember when I played a 2nd XI game for Lancashire for the first time, I got a brown envelope at the end of the game with about £50 pounds in it, and I thought, "This will do for me."

You started to make a name for yourself as a teenager playing in the Lancashire leagues. What are your memories of this period?

I played for Dutton Forshaw and I had been there since I was a really young kid. I then moved to St Anne's to try and further my career. I got offers to go to private school on scholarships, but from the age of 10, I was playing against adults and my Dad played as well. My Mum was keen for me to go to private school, but in the end I didn't go. I started playing for the 4th team at St Anne's with my brother Chris, and they got us mixed up. He was meant to be doing the batting and I was meant to be doing the bowling but he got 6 wickets and I got 50! I then played in the 2nd team, and then quickly got into the first team. I remember my debut in the first team was against Netherfield who had Kenny Benjamin, the West Indian fast bowler, playing for them which was not pleasant. The lad opening the batting for us got stretchered off after being hit on the head whilst trying to get out the way of a bouncer and put his back out. I was bricking myself when I went in to bat, as I was only 14 at the time.

How old were you when you knew that cricket was going to be your livelihood?

It was probably after I had played that second-team game for Lancashire at the age of 15. I was studying at school at the time, preparing for GCSEs, and my original thoughts were to go to college and then university, but when I played that game and got paid for it, I gave my Dad the petrol money and kept the rest for myself. I realised then that I could earn a living from it. Bumble [David Lloyd, then Lancashire head coach] came round to my house and told me what people could earn. At the time, he was talking about £16,000 and all our faces lit up. It was a great opportunity. I knew I wanted to do it, so my schoolwork just came to a halt, because I knew I was going to leave school at 16. I got offered a three-year contract by Lancashire, and I have been there ever since.

You made your debut, aged 17, playing in a Lancashire side full of stars. This must have been an exciting time for you?

I played my first game against the Minor Counties at Leek in a one-day game. I managed to get 1 for 10, but I was gutted because Bumble batted me down at number 10. I couldn't complain though as I was batting behind Jason Gallian, John Crawley and all these lads. I played my first first-class game at Portsmouth against Hampshire. Bumble had told everyone that I was unbelievable in the slips, so I had to field second slip and one of the senior pros, Neil Fairbrother I think, got nudged out - and I dropped three catches off Wasim Akram! I actually questioned whether I was good enough at that stage, as I got 9 in the first innings and a duck in the second. I bowled quickly, but my back went. I've never been very good at debuts. I was just quiet and wouldn't say boo to a goose.

Who was the biggest single influence in helping you get there?

My Dad, without a doubt. There were others, coaches and people I played with, but my father instilled in me his love of cricket, but it was never forced on me. As a kid, he drove me around all over the country. My brother helped me as well to some degree. Being younger than Chris, I found that I wanted to keep up with him and I think that helped me. Chris was good. At a young age, he was probably better than me. But he was never that fussed. He was more academic, but he gave me a lot of support as well, especially when I started playing for Lancashire.

What was the big breakthrough moment in your career?

I suppose it was when I scored a hundred for the second team at Lancashire when I was 15. Initially, they were going to offer me a two-year contract but, after that hundred, they upped it to three years. At first, I blew a bit hot and cold, going up and down between the first and second teams, which was a bit of a theme for me in my early days. Later on in my career though, I got a serious dressing down from Chubby Chandler and Neil Fairbrother. My career was going nowhere. Although I had played for England, I wasn't performing well, I was only getting 30 or 40 every time. I was fat and unfit. I was lucky to be playing for Lancashire, never mind England. The riot act was read to me in the dressing-room at Old Trafford. From there, we devised a plan as to how I was going to get back into the England side. I went to the Academy and was then given a lifeline by being picked for the one-day squad to tour Zimbabwe. I did well on that trip and got a late call-up to tour India as a bowler.

You made your debut for England in 1998. Yet it took five years for you to reach a point where you were an automatic pick in the side. How difficult is it to break into the side and then fully establish yourself?

Breaking into the England side came quite easily, probably too easily in some ways. I made my debut aged 20 and I had only been bowling for a few weeks. At every level I have played at, county cricket and international cricket, I have always struggled and taken time to settle. Once I realised that I was good enough to be there, and was confident enough, things were fine. Everyone saw me as that person in the middle having a laugh, but there were insecurities there as well and that was something I had to deal with.

Confidence is a word you hear so often in sport. When you have spells when you are out of form and low on confidence, how do you go about regaining it?

People have various ways of coping with this. Obviously sports psychologists are used, for example, but I think it has to come from within. I have used psychologists in the past and it has worked for a period, but you have got to find your own way of regaining form. For me, it is keeping the game in perspective and enjoying it. If I am not enjoying it, then I won't perform. The two things go hand in hand. When you go out to bat and you are out of form, you just see fielders. When you go out to bat and are in form, you just see the gaps. You might have to kid yourself sometimes, but the main thing is enjoyment and having a perspective on it. My dips in form have mainly come through injury. Whenever I have played my best cricket, I have got injured soon afterwards. That has been a theme for me. As soon as I found that I have got somewhere fitness-wise, form-wise, it gets taken away and I am back to square one, back on my crutches.

In the first Ashes Test at Lord's in 2005, you scored 0 and 3. In the next Test at Edgbaston, you scored 68 and 73. In between these games, you met a sports psychologist. What advice did he give you?

We sat down and had a chat. He said that I was just putting too much pressure on myself. You are always going to get pressure from outside, but it's the pressure you put on yourself that you feel. So I got away from the game for a few days and came back and decided that, if I was going to fail, I was going to do it on my terms; not cower down, but to go out and give it a swing. He told me to go out and express myself – and it came off.

You captained England in India in the 2006 series where you performed with bat and ball and received great praise from the media for your stewardship of a young and inexperienced side. How much did you enjoy this experience?

The captaincy was good. I was playing well, I was fit, scoring runs and taking wickets. If anything needed doing, I felt I could do it myself. I enjoyed the responsibility of captaining a young side, and there wasn't a great deal expected of this young team in India. This allowed us to just go out and play. We nearly won the first Test and should never have lost the second. In Mumbai, we turned it around and won a Test match there for the first time in over 20 years. It was as good as it gets. That achievement was as big as anything.

The Ashes 2006/7 series in Australia was a difficult time for everyone in the England team. As captain, how tough a period was this for you, having previously experienced such highs against Australia?

It was the toughest time in my career. I didn't know how to deal with it. There was nothing I could do and I went into myself, into my shell. The thing about captaincy is it can be great, but it is tough. I found it hard to express my feelings, in my way, as a captain. With someone like Michael Vaughan, he just keeps his feelings constant all the time. I wasn't able to do that. I couldn't escape it in the evenings, I couldn't just switch off; it was on my mind all the time. At that point, I realised that I maybe wasn't the captain I wanted to be and it was probably one job too many.

What was the defining moment in your career; the day you would pick out as being the most important?

It's hard to say, as there are a lot of things that happen throughout your career. When I scored my first Test century, I was going in on a pair in the second innings, yet somehow I got a hundred and I came off at tea and couldn't believe that I had just got a Test hundred. That's when the penny started to drop. There were Ashes wins and performances in other games. And I enjoyed playing under Vaughany. He gave me confidence and knew how to get the best out of me. For the three years building up to 2005, that was when I was at my best.

Do you think you can control your mind?

Not fully, no. I have seen research that says that you only use about 3% of your mind or something silly, so can I control it? No, I don't think so. When I am on the cricket field and have a ball in my hand, I can run up and know exactly what I am going to bowl. Once it has left my hand though, it's out of my control. As a batter, I can't control what the bowler is going to deliver, but I can control my emotion. However, it's not something I have really thought of before, but there have been times when I have controlled games.

What do you feel is your most destructive emotion and how do you deal with it?

Like most sportsmen, insecurity. At some point, you will question yourself. It's something you just have to deal with. Past experiences and past performances can go some way towards dealing with it. I just try to put some perspective on the situation. I have experienced injuries, poor form, a 5-nil defeat in the Ashes – and it can't get any worse than that - so in terms of what I have been through, I won't say that you can't hurt me, but I am just here to enjoy myself.

What do you do when you feel nervous?

I try to hide it. You're always going to get nerves. When I walk out to bat with my helmet on and look around, I am nervous. But nerves are a sign for me that you care about what you are doing. It's also a sign that you are ready to play. It depends on what sort of tag you put on it. For me, it means I'm here and I'm ready. When you stand there waiting for that first ball with someone like Brett Lee or Shoaib Akhtar coming up to bowl, it makes you feel alive, it's great. If I get a boundary away early, I'm happy. I've been a bad starter from time to time and have had a lot of ducks, so once I have got off the mark or got a boundary in the first few balls, then I'm usually away.

What is the best example of your being at your very best?

Batting against the West Indies at Edgbaston in 2004, when I got my highest Test score of 167. I went through a period at that time when I just knew I would score runs. There was no doubt at all, I was just walking out and scoring runs. It was like that for about two to three years.

What do you dislike about your sport?

Sometimes the lifestyle and the travel can get to you. My body isn't conducive to what I do, what with the rigours I have to go through to bowl and the strains and stresses it puts on my body. That's probably the hardest thing for me.

At what point in your career did you realise that hard work and preparation off the field paid massive dividends on it?

It was when Chubby and Neil gave me that bollocking in the dressing-room aged 23. I think I always knew what the problem was, but I needed someone to tell me. It was good to get it out in the open and hear it from people who were close to me and people I respected. After that, the penny dropped and it was all about performing and getting back into the England side.

To what degree can a sportsperson learn from the people around them and who were the people that gave you the best advice?

I'm fortunate that I play a team game, so I always have people around me for help, expertise and confidence. Growing up, I go back to my father and a coach called Jim Kenyon who helped me between the ages of 11 and 15, and then David Lloyd when he was at Lancashire. Then there's the dressing room, with people such as Neil Fairbrother, Wasim Akram, Peter Martin, Glen Chapple. You can reel off all the names. I have been fortunate to have those sorts of people around me. Neil Fairbrother is now my manager, and I have a close relationship with my physio Rooster (Dave Roberts) and my family. I don't think it's any coincidence that the upturn in my career coincided with me meeting my wife Rachael. She is very driven and that has rubbed off on me.

What's been the most important ingredient in your achieving success?

I've enjoyed it. All I ever wanted to do was play, and fortunately I've been able to do that. Also, when I have been injured and the game is taken away from you, you realise what it means, and how much you want to get back - and that has been the driving force behind all the rehab as well.

What would you do differently if you had your time again?

I don't know. I get asked this question a lot. You have regrets of course, but whatever I have done has made me what I am today. I'll be stubborn and say I wouldn't do a great deal differently. I'd have maybe not played a few shots and there were other issues off the field as well, but all that has made me come back from various injuries. It's given me the strength to do it. I have gone through some hard times, but it's not been boring. It's been a bit of a roller-coaster really, but I'm still here.

What would you like to do when you finish playing?

I don't know. I'm enjoying spending time with the family at the moment, so I'd like to do more of that. Over the next few years, whilst I am still playing, as I am only playing Twenty20s and one-day games, it will give me opportunities to explore other avenues. So when the day comes when I can't play any longer, there will be a natural transition into something else, as opposed to some players, when they finish playing, they don't know what they are doing. I've had offers of various things, but it would have to be something that excites me.

What one-line sentence would you give to anybody aspiring to be the best they could be?

You have to enjoy what you do. Otherwise there is no point, especially in sport.

Which sportsman or sportswoman do you admire the most and why?

Of all the people I have met, I still get excited about meeting cricketers. I grew up watching Ian Botham – and now I spend time with him. Sachin Tendulkar too. And I've met Sir Garfield Sobers also. When I meet these people, I am like a kid. I've met various people from other sports and don't feel like that. From other sports, I admire Lawrence Dallaglio for his pride and his passion. When I was younger, I used to like Mike Tyson; he just took on the world and was an unbelievable fighter.

KARL MORRIS SUMMARY

None of us should ever underestimate the power of words. It can be a single word, a sentence or a full-blown conversation. Make no mistake though, words DO change lives. It could well be that one of the finest cricketers and most inspirational figures may have ended up relatively unknown were it not for the conversation that Andrew Flintoff had with his manager Andrew Chandler and Neil Fairbrother.

It is clear those words that day had such an impact on a career that appeared to be drifting along towards obscurity. Words guide us, direct us and motivate us. Do you coach? Do you teach? Are you a parent? Choose your words VERY wisely, as at a young age, the comments from an authority figure can literally alter the path of life of a young person.

Throughout this book, the passion for an individual and his or her sport is apparent, and it is clear that the love of cricket was instilled by Andrew's father at a very early age. Andrew loved to PLAY cricket. Let us not forget within these pages that all of the motivational talk and encouragement HAS to be underpinned by a deep love of playing the game for its own sake.

Andrew may not have worked formally on the mental game to any great extent, but some of the phrases he uses could come straight from a user's guide to effective psychology. "When the ball leaves my hand there is nothing I can do and there is no control over the kind of ball I receive from the opposition," is a mindset that focuses on what HE can control, as opposed to concerning himself too much with things he has no influence on whatsoever.

Also, to say that the game can't hurt him much more is a very effective strategy. We will all suffer setbacks and defeats, the key thing is we CAN overcome almost anything that sport and life throw at us with the right attitude. With this mindset, we can begin to see that the 'worst that can happen' is not the end of the world. A very wise man once said that "those who aren't afraid to lose are also not afraid to win." Andrew Flintoff has failed occasionally, but it is a testament to the man himself that we all remember his glorious successes. His legacy will stand the test of time and, for those of us who have seen him at his best, we must consider ourselves extremely lucky.

DR JANET GRAY, MBE

Dr Janet Gray MBE was born on 16th August 1962 in Belfast, Northern Ireland and was educated at Seaview Primary School and Greymount Girls' School. As a schoolgirl and throughout her teenage years, she led a very happy life and was a confident, bubbly and independent person. Aged 21, her life was turned upside down. Janet lost her sight. Confronted by a terrifying new world, in which her courage and resolve were tested to the full, she amazingly discovered the world of water skiing. This new love, combined with her tenacious character, saw her win the World Disabled Championship in all three disciplines and she was World Champion in 1999, 2001 and 2003. But her courage was to be tested yet again.

A horrific accident came close to killing her. In 2004, during a practice session in America, she struck a steel jump-ramp at the speed of 40mph. The force of the impact was such that the doctors had all but written her off, but after three years of intensive rehabilitation - not to mention countless operations - astoundingly, she took to her skis again. Her renaissance was confirmed when she won the 2007 World Championships in Australia.

QUESTIONS

How would you describe your childhood?

I had a very happy childhood. I was always a very bubbly, outgoing, sporty individual – a happy-go-lucky sort of child and very independent.

To what degree was sport a part of your life?

Swimming played a big part in my life when I was growing up; I had an affinity with water and was always attracted to it. When I was very young, my grandmother was petrified that I would fall in somewhere when we were on holidays. So we were given swimming lessons and I just loved it. We lived close to a pool and I got heavily involved with swimming and then lifesaving. I was much happier in water than out of it. I was never very co-ordinated with racquet sports and I didn't have good hand-eye co-ordination either.

You were 21-years old, happy and independent. Then you lost your sight. What happened?

Unfortunately, a very rare strain of glaucoma runs in my family; my father had lost his sight through it. The experts said that it wasn't possible that it was hereditary, that it wouldn't be passed on and that it was more of an unfortunate accident that it happened to my father. But they never really got to the bottom of why it happened to him. My parents were advised that having children would be fine. Unfortunately, that wasn't the case. My brother Ian lost his sight at the age of 12. At that stage, the doctors began to monitor my eyesight and unfortunately I developed the same condition and lost my sight at the age of 21.

Can you describe how you felt in the first few days and weeks following this?

It was absolutely terrifying. I went into surgery in order to try to save some of the sight but I woke up without any – and it was just horrific. It's utter disbelief that you feel and I just hoped and prayed that, post surgery, it would settle down, the blood would clear, the sight would come back and everything would be fine. You live in hope, but there was also an awful dread. It just shatters your whole world. 90% of life is visual, so when you lose this major sense, you are just so vulnerable. I had driven the day before, I had my independence and then suddenly I couldn't move. I couldn't dash across a room or just run off somewhere without thinking about it. Everything was so alien – a totally alien environment, and a petrifying one.

What was the hardest part of losing your sight?

Losing my independence, having to depend on others and not being able to drive anymore. Just not being able to just get up and go out somewhere was extremely difficult to deal with. Not having independence was a massive thing.

How frightening was this?

It was terrifying. Suddenly your world goes completely black. You're plunged into this awful world of darkness. You're disorientated and you bump into things, which is totally draining – and of course you have to rely on others. It's a horrible place to be. Believe me, sighted people should never take their sight for granted. You don't have to rely on your other senses, such as your sense of touch. Suddenly not being able to see something and then having to start to actually feel it, it's a horrible place to be. Not good.

Was there a moment when you started to accept that you had a new life without your sight?

I don't think there was a defining moment. I think it was a case of going through shock, disbelief, anguish, terror and then finally coming to the realisation that this was how life was going to be. I wasn't going to get any sight back. Aged 21, my life was really only just beginning and then suddenly, I had the feeling that it had ended. I became very ill. I am 5feet 8inches tall and my weight plummeted to 5 stone 10 pounds, just from the sheer shock and trauma of it all. In that situation, you slip into a spiral of weight loss; are in and out of hospital; have no mental reserves; and are vulnerable to catching every disease going. I developed a series of chest infections and the cycle seemed never-ending. You don't know how you are going to get out of the awful hole you are in. But you have to keep on going and I always kept myself busy. When I lost my sight, I had just got married and moved into a new home. I busied myself with all the renovations in the home; I cleaned the house from top to bottom, then just started it all over again, so that I didn't have time to think about the situation I was in. Thinking about it was something I just totally avoided.

How did you then come across water skiing?

My husband Paul had been a water skier but had injured his Achilles tendon, which meant he had to give up the sport. We thought nothing more about it but one day, a few years later, Paul's uncle asked him to come down to the lake for a ski and I went with him. I was just happy to be around water. I had imagined that participation in sport for me had ended, as I thought I couldn't possibly do sport as a blind person. We went to the lake and I went out in the boat and it was all very exciting. I was then asked if I would like to try and I said yes. The following weekend, I took my swimming gear and I found that I was really excited for the first time in quite a while.

What did this excitement feel like?

It was awesome. You don't realise what doors are going to open and how they can change your life. I got into the correct position - which Paul showed me - and I just followed his instructions. Once the ropes tightened, Paul said "Hit it!" I did exactly what he said; he grabbed me by the top of the life jacket; said that I could stand up; and that was it. Just standing up and realising that I was on top of the water, that I had got up for the first time and that I was actually skiing, was just absolutely amazing and we went around the lake about three times. I just couldn't believe it. It was a wonderful feeling of achievement. Of course, the second time I went out I wanted to do it on my own, as I felt I didn't need Paul beside me. It was then that I realised that here was a sport which I could do as a blind person and something which I could enjoy. The freedom of being on the end of the rope just like any sighted skier gave me back a little something of that independence that I had lost. That's what attracted me to it – the sheer exhilaration of it. There was the rush and speed - it was such an exciting, extreme sort of sport. It opened a whole new world for me, which was the big turning-point.

When you are on the water and the boat is pulling you at 35 mph, what are you seeing in your mind or are you concentrating on the feel of the water and your interaction with it?

You need total concentration. You use all your senses: your hearing, your touch, the water beneath you. You listen for the boat engine, you listen for signals. Your senses are in overdrive. As you accelerate, the pull across the wake gives you a tremendous sense of exhilaration. You get that lovely swing which is what you are aiming for.

What elements are involved in water skiing?

There are three different disciplines in waterskiing: slalom, tricks and jump. I learnt to slalom and trick when I started at the beginning. Paul had always maintained that it was crazy for blind people to jump and he was insistent that I should never do it. Nevertheless, I was eventually encouraged to try it at Heron Lake, the National Disabled Water Ski Centre. When I went over the ramp for the first time and landed, I was so excited that I just let go of the rope. The second time around I landed and skied away. At the end of the week's training you had to pass an exam, needing to land three competent jumps out of three.

How did it feel to become World Champion?

It was awesome. The World Championships were held six weeks later at Heron Lake, where I had just learnt to jump. I had the confidence that I knew the ramp, that I could land and that everything would be OK. I had hoped to get through to the finals but I went in with the attitude that I had nothing to lose, being relatively inexperienced and the new girl on the block. When I won the wake slalom, I couldn't believe it. I then won the audio slalom and I also won silver medals in the jumps and tricks. That gave me the most points, making me the overall winner. It was so unexpected, as it all just happened.

Was this a liberating landmark to have reached?

Yes, absolutely. But you have to learn to look forward and not spend too much time looking back. And you have to make the most of what you have. Until I became World Champion, it had just been a hobby. It was great to be the best in the world, but I realised that to stay at the top I would need to work twice as hard, as you can't rest on your laurels. So the hobby then changed into a career. I got on a funding programme with Sport Northern Ireland and the Government. I sat down with a team and developed a proper training and coaching plan. It was a whole new regime and a whole new way of life.

Do you have a set routine for mentally preparing for an event?

Getting mental preparation right is a trial and error process; you have to work out what works for you and what doesn't. I have also tried visualisation, but I find that mentally visualising everything doesn't seem to help. For me, what works is putting in the hours training, with preparation time on the water making sure everything is fine, followed by total relaxation and trying to stay calm. And I also make sure I enjoy it! I find that the harder I try, the more worked up I get. The more worked up I get, the more I panic and I suddenly get myself into this awful spiral, so I have had to learn to take a step back, relax and realise that whatever will happen, will happen. It's trying to find that mix of total concentration and yet not working too hard, staying relaxed so that it all flows naturally.

Is there a one-line expression you tell yourself whilst competing to drive you on?

I tell myself that I know what has to be done, so let's go and do it.

Do you think you can control your mind?

Yes, I do. I think the mind is the most powerful thing we possess.

How do you deal with doubt?

I doubt myself a lot. I don't know whether it's because I don't have my sight, but for me my memory is everything. As a blind person, you work out your system for everything around the home. The most frustrating thing is when you put something down and either you don't remember where you have put it or someone comes along and moves it. That just drives you insane. The total vulnerability of being blind does lead you to doubt yourself. It's like getting up in pitch darkness and tripping over something on the way to the bathroom. For me, that's a permanent way of living. You have to have ground-rules, but you learn the hard way. Any door in the house you either have left fully open or properly closed; you never leave it ajar. With cupboard doors, it's a must. You take out what you want and then you shut the door; you never leave it open. I need to concentrate a lot when I am ironing – once you've burnt your hands a couple of times, you soon learn and your memory becomes photographic. I had my sight for 21 years, so I can visualise things very quickly. At least I know what colours are. I do doubt myself, but now that I have got my mind trained, the doubts aren't there in everyday living. When it comes to competition, there can be doubts, so I have to hit an override button which tells me 'I have trained for this; I know I can do it'. You always have to keep the positive thoughts coming.

What do you do when you feel nervous?

Everyone gets nervous. If you don't get nervous, you lose that adrenalin-rush and that is something you need. I've discovered that when I get nervous before a competition, it's best to stay away from the dock and just go around and chat to everyone and try to have a laugh because I know what I have to do. My preparation is all done. By then, it's just a case of going out and doing it.

When you are under extreme pressure, how do you deal with that?

In the 2003 World Championships, I tied for first place in the slalom final and it went to a ski-off. I'd won the 1999 and 2001 Championships and I wasn't going to give it up without a fight. Rather than going out at my normal speed of 52 kph, I decided to go off at 55 kph. I just told myself to go out and win it with the world record. Once I had made that decision in my mind, it was a case of going out there and doing it. I had an absolute feeling of relief when I heard the double bleep at the end of that pass, knowing that Suzy, the girl I was skiing off against, had missed her run.

What makes a bad day?

It depends so much on the weather. Windy conditions aren't good because it can get dangerous. Heavy rain isn't good either. A bad day is when you go out and have a bad jump when you may land on your head and get a bit of a fright - that can certainly shake you up.

What's been the most important ingredient in achieving your success?

In a word, support. My husband Paul has been absolutely fabulous; I have had great support and encouragement from him. He's been the one behind me pushing me all the way. I've also had very good support from the Sports Institute in Northern Ireland.

What one-line sentence would you give to anybody aspiring to be the best they could be?

I would tell them to set their ultimate goal, keep their focus, be determined, dedicated and totally committed. They then need to break the pathway down into bite-size and achievable goals. So long as they remain focused and committed, they will achieve their ultimate goal.

What advice can you give to anyone who suffers a similar setback to yourself?

Don't look back; you have to look forward. Looking back is dangerous. Rumination leads to ruination. You can't hanker after what has been, because it's gone. It's in the past and life has changed. You have to assess the situation you are in and then make the most of it.

Have you set yourself any other major goals for the future?

After competitive life, I would like to go full time into after-dinner, motivational and inspirational speaking. I'm looking forward to working with young people in sport and further developing the sport of water skiing in Northern Ireland. I hope that my own book, *Blind Ambition* will inspire others.

Which sportsman or sportswoman from another sport do you admire the most and why?

I very much admire Lance Armstrong. I can empathise with him in so many ways. How he fought back from cancer and was determined to get back, which he did. He's a tremendous example and a great role-model.

Blind Ambition published by Gill & Macmillan (October 2009)

KARL MORRIS SUMMARY

Seldom, in all of the time that I have been involved in sport, have I ever heard such an inspiring and truly motivational story as the one related by Dr Janet Gray. Her words of wisdom should be required reading for every athlete, participant, parent or businessperson. In a few sentences you have the definitive example of mental toughness.

Here is a person who was robbed at an early age of the most precious of human gifts, her sight. Yet, she tells a story of overcoming incredible odds to achieve spectacular success.

However, let us not be drawn too much into the emotion of the story. I am sure Janet would like us to look at the key points we can ALL learn from and apply in our own personal quest for self-mastery and achievement.

As I will state throughout this book, success leaves behind a trail. There are certain ingredients which seem to keep reappearing with successful people. This is across sport and across almost all walks of life. It would have been so easy for Janet to wallow in self-pity, but what strikes me first of all about her is the word PASSION.

She describes the passion as a child of being in water. The sheer joy that swimming gave her as a youngster was temporarily halted with the onset of blindness. Yet, this was a passion which would not go away. The opportunity to reignite that passion came with the chance to water ski.

Ask yourself:

What are YOU passionate about?

What is it that truly gives you pleasure just for the sheer joy of doing the activity for its own sake?

When we are involved in something for its own sake, as opposed to the external rewards it might bring, we get close to our own personal potential for peak experience. It is incredibly important you seek out that which gives you a feeling of intense pleasure in the activity itself.

Far too often, people live a life which is without this true passion; and this is both a waste and a tragedy.

91

It may come from business, it may come from sport or it may come from your family, but I believe we ALL need to seek out this fire that burns within us. When we can light that flame, we will stop at nothing to become what we are truly capable of being. Janet's story is an extreme example of this.

We also learn from Janet about the importance of quality preparation to give us confidence. Far too often these days for my own liking, we are fed messages such as 'think positive' or 'believe in yourself'. It is important to understand it is NOT all in the mind. To develop true and lasting confidence, we do need to develop the twin-set of confidence and competence.

Sitting under a tree and visualizing yourself as successful will have little or no impact if you do not have the skills to match. To know you are fully prepared is THE most effective tool to developing mental toughness and self-belief. It is vital to understand what is the RIGHT preparation for you personally. This is why we all need coaches and mentors to assist us on the way as guides and sounding boards.

"Rumination leads to ruination." We should all look at that sentence every day and emblazon it in our hearts and minds. Clearly, from what you have read above, a truly tough mind does not dwell on the past. The past IS over - it will not come back no matter how much we wish for it. Yet, Dr Janet Gray is an outstanding example of someone who truly has the courage and conviction to look forward. In circumstances so dreadful that most people thankfully will never experience, she demonstrates the incredible power of being able to look forward, set passionate goals and be involved on a daily basis in the adventure of making things come true.

ALAN HANSEN

Alan David Hansen was born on 13th June 1955 in Sauchie, Clackmannanshire, Scotland and was educated at Lornshill Academy in Alloa. He is a former football player and, for more than a decade now, he has been the BBC's main football pundit. Beginning his career at Partick Thistle, he then moved to Liverpool for £110,000 in 1977. In the following 14 years, Hansen played 620 games and scored 14 times for the club. This was during the most successful period in the history of Liverpool FC, when Hansen won three European Cups, eight League Championships, two FA Cups and four League Cups. In the 1986 season, with Hansen as captain, Liverpool completed a League and FA Cup double. He also played 26 times for Scotland and retired from the sport in 1991.

QUESTIONS

What's your first football memory?

I can remember kicking a ball when I was about two years old. My brother played and if he played football, I'd play football. I remember at the old house, kicking the ball against the wall – and that's what I did in the formative years. I would kick the ball against that wall until I started playing for Partick, when I was 17. Between the ages of five and 14, I used to come back from school at 4 o'clock, and immediately start kicking the ball against that wall. And doing it non-stop for hours and hours, by myself – left foot, right foot, left foot, right foot. Then on Saturdays and Sundays we used to play football in the parks. We used to put jackets or jumpers down and it was 55-a-side and everyone played because in those days there was nothing else. Even if you didn't like football, you still played. There were no computers, no PlayStations. And I never got tired of it. I never thought, "I'm not going to do that today." It was what I did, and that's how I learnt to play the game.

Who introduced you to the game?

My Dad was an amateur player, so I suppose it was him. The first time I ever played in a team was at primary school, aged six. When I went to secondary school, you had a team for every year: Under 12s, Under 13s and Under 14s. Then, when I was fourteen, I played for the boys' club, who were Under 16s. So, I played on Saturday mornings at school and Saturday afternoons for the boys' club.

Can you remember the first game you watched at a stadium?

I remember going to see Scotland play Austria at Hampden Park sometime in the early 1960s. I went with the school and it was the first time I had gone to a floodlit match. It was mesmeric. I remember going up the steps at Hampden and coming to the entrance where the seats were and looking at the pitch with the floodlights on it, and it was a joy to behold. I can't remember the score. I can't remember anything about the game, I just remember the floodlights and thinking "how good is this?" and it was a great moment.

At junior level, you represented Scotland in volleyball, squash and golf. You must have been playing sport every day?

I'd never even seen a squash-court in my life before I went to Lornshill Academy and there was a squash-court right in the middle of the school. When I got to the sixth form, I wasn't going to classes, I was playing squash for five or six hours every day. I was obviously relatively fit and I had good eye-to-ball co-ordination and I was very competitive too. I wanted to win every time I went on the court. And squash gave me added fitness which gave me an advantage when I was playing football.

At what point did the football start to take over?

I was a very good golfer when I was young – I had a handicap of 2 when I was 15, and had maintained that when I was 17. But I knew I was never going to be good enough to make a living out of playing golf, so I started concentrating on my football. When I left school, I had decided to go to Aberdeen University to read history, and someone said, "You play all these sports. You should be a PE teacher". So I went for the interview at PE College but didn't get in for one reason or another, and I was left in limbo. But I knew Partick Thistle wanted me to play for them, so that's what I did. And the rest, as they say, is history.

So your real ambition was to be a professional golfer?

Yes, always. Golf has always been my first love and always will be. I started playing golf when I was 7. In the winter I would go back to playing football, but in the summers I would be at Alloa Golf Course in Sauchie, morning, noon and night. I wouldn't go home. The golf-course was only 150 yards away from the house, so I would be there all day.

Aged 15, you had a trial at Liverpool, but were told that you were not good enough. How did that make you feel?

I was invited to play in a game at Melwood. I played out of position in the middle of the park and I never saw the ball. I just remember people flying in and kicking me. I went back home and when I got the letter to say that I wasn't good enough, I was really pleased because there was no way I wanted to go to Liverpool at that time. I wanted to stay in Scotland. So I was happy.

At the age of 18 then, with your golfing ambitions left behind, at what level were you playing football?

When I was younger, I could have gone to a number of other clubs in Scotland, but Partick were the first ones to offer me terms when I was 18. I played a game for Sauchie juniors against Partick and after the game, the Partick manager came up to me and said, "Right, have you made your mind up? Are you going to come and play for us?" and I said "OK, I will" and that was it. I signed a contract.

When was it clear that you were going to make it professionally?

In my mind, I have always been a bit insecure. I had always been told that I was the best junior football-player there had ever been in the region, but I never took any notice of that. As I only ever wanted to play golf, it didn't matter what they said. One problem I had was that, because I was tall for my age, (I was 6ft 2ins when I was 16), I was always tired. Some people thought this was because I was out on the drink, but it was growing problems. I just grew too quickly. My son has suffered the same issues with height and tiredness. But as I got older, the problem seemed to sort itself out. Going into the Partick dressing-room for the first time was a real education. In the four years I played at Partick, the biggest thing I learnt was not how to play football, but how to be mentally quick in the dressing-room. It could sometimes be cynical and brutal and if you weren't sharp, then you'd get hammered. At first, as an 18-year-old, it was torture. I never knew whether I was coming or going. It was an education about everything, about life. Fortunately for me, I started to adapt to the quicker pace of the game and, even against the better players, I just became better and better. Eventually, the problems with me getting tired went and, significantly, I went from being a midfield player into a centre back, my best position.

Who was the biggest single influence in helping you get to this point in your career?

I played in a certain style and nobody tried to say to me that I couldn't do this or I couldn't do that, that's not the way to play. All my coaches knew I had an individual style of playing. I never had a mentor at Partick; I never looked up to anyone. My brother was five years older than me but I never asked him for advice. I've always been the same. I go it alone. I was a solitary figure. I'd be right in the mix when it came to the laughing, joking and the wind-ups, but when it came to looking for support, I usually sorted things out myself. This is what Joe Fagan said when I had a bad three months at Liverpool in 1982/3. Joe became Liverpool manager in 1984. He'd been there as a coach so he knew me inside out. I knew I was having a bad spell, and Joe wrote later that there was no way he was going to try to tell me anything. He knew I could sort it out for myself, so he just left me alone. And that was really good judgement. If I was ever having a bad time at any stage in my career, I would try to look after myself better. I wouldn't go out, I wouldn't drink, I'd try and eat sensibly until I got back to where I was. No-one ever told me to do that. I did it myself.

What was your big breakthrough moment?

My big breakthrough moment was my debut for Liverpool at Anfield. There were 54,000 inside the ground and 10,000 outside. It was completely different from anything I'd experienced at Partick, even when we played against Celtic or Rangers. Three or four weeks after my debut, we played Everton in a derby match at Anfield. The feelings I had when I heard the crescendo of noise coming out of the tunnel is something that I will never experience again in my life. That day at Anfield, with that noise coming out of the tunnel, it was just unbelievable. You could not hear yourself think. It was incredible. And it scared me a bit. I was scared I wasn't good enough. And I was homesick. I really wanted to be in Scotland, so that didn't help. But after about 18 months, I gradually got to grips with things, and I felt better.

What sacrifices have you had to make in order to achieve success?

If you have kids, Christmas is always a difficult time, as there is always a game on Boxing Day. On Christmas morning we would have to train from 10.30am until 11.30am, then back again at 3.30pm. So, you'd only have between 12pm and 3pm with your kids, which is hard. Bob Paisley [Liverpool manager from 1974-1983] always said we should have Christmas in the summer. I suppose that's the attitude you should have as a professional if you've got kids. In the last season I played, my children were 9 and 6 and it was tough when you've got to leave as soon as they've got their presents. But that's the sort of sacrifice you have to make at the highest level. There was never any compassion, never any extra hours. The game tomorrow was more important than Christmas Day. This was Liverpool. This was about winning. Have your Christmas in the summer.

If there was one piece of advice that helped you become successful, what was it?

What I learnt more than anything else at Liverpool – and this might not go down well with everybody – was that winning is everything. That was the philosophy at Liverpool. And they weren't interested in how we won; it was just, win the match and worry about how you played later. The great line at Liverpool was "first is first, second is nowhere". Joe Fagan and Bob Paisley were strong preachers of that message. I can remember sitting in the dressing-room after winning the European Cup as a 22-year-old sipping a glass of champagne, when Joe Fagan came in and said, "Congratulations on winning the European Cup, but it's been a disappointing season." And we'd just won the European Cup! He said that the First Division Championship was our bread and butter and we had finished eight points behind the winners, Nottingham Forest. The club wanted us to do better. So the next year, we won the First Division Championship, with a record number of points, a record number of goals scored, a record for the least number of goals conceded and I remember Joe coming into the dressing room after winning the Championship and he said there would be no lap of honour, no gala dinner. He just said, "That was better." What he was doing, of course, was instilling in us a policy that if you slip from your high standards, and let complacency in, that was the way to failure. And that's what Manchester United teams think now. If you think you've arrived and if you think you don't need to do the hard work and if you think you don't need to have all the attributes which made you successful, you'll fail. Success is the easy part; maintaining success is the hard part. You have to keep evolving, you have to keep improving, individually and collectively, to continue to succeed.

Did you have a set routine for mentally preparing before each game?

Yes – going through purgatory! I was always terrible beforehand. It's a bit like broadcasting, where the nerves are always there beforehand. I've never been nervous on a football pitch in my life but beforehand, I was like a nervous wreck. Going down the tunnel was like a release. All nerves disappeared, and then after the game I would have a drink and think, what were those pre-match nerves all about? But as I got older, the worse it got beforehand. The nerves were unbelievable. I was thinking we might get beaten, we might play badly, we might struggle; everything and anything which was negative. But the great thing was that when I got on the pitch, all I thought about was winning. I suppose what I needed was a psychiatrist. The fear of losing was obviously good for me; the fear of getting beaten actually helped me.

Do you think you can control your mind?

I think certain people can. I can control my mind to a certain extent, but I can't control fear or worry. If I'd been able to control it, then I wouldn't have been so nervous before each match. It's like on a Saturday when I do *Match of the Day* now. I get edgy and nervous but when I go on screen, I haven't got a nerve in my body. It's an amazing feeling. At 9pm when we are ready to go, I am fine. But during the day, that's when I get all the nerves.

What do you feel is your most destructive emotion and how do you deal with it?

My most destructive emotion is fear. The fear of doing badly. It used to be the fear of losing, but now it's fear of doing badly. The perception that people might think, oh he's gone a bit. That's basically like when you get past 30 in football. Because you go past 30, people automatically look at the number, 31, 32, 33 and say he's gone.

What is the best example of you being at your very best?

As a player, I had different kinds of performance levels to my career. Before I was about 28 years old, I was unbelievably quick and athletic and could run all day. Then I went into a second phase, where I couldn't do as many forward runs, but I was more experienced. There is a phrase that says "experience is everything" and I was definitely a better player when I got to my 30s. I couldn't do what I was doing when I was 24, but I had a lot of experience and I had the knowledge of how to play centre-back. Although I had some bad periods from time to time, (the '82/'83 season comes to mind), on the whole my consistency levels were astonishing. That was because I knew how to play centre-back inside out. I had it down to a fine art – and obviously I was playing in a great team with great players. Most professional footballers experience a tailing-off in their careers in their last couple of years, but the last game I ever played for Liverpool was when I lifted the League Championship in 1990 – so I went out on the biggest high. At the age of 35, I had had a phenomenal season, so it was a hell of a way to finish. That was great. Individually, and as part of a team, that was such a great time.

What do you dislike about your sport?

I really dislike people who talk about how the game should be played. But that's not a hatred; it's just my opinion. If you look at the way Wimbledon played in the 1980s when they were not very sophisticated and were physically intimidating, to me that was just playing to their strengths, and there's nothing wrong with that. Bob Paisley would agree with that, I'm sure. You play to your strengths and expose everyone else's weaknesses. If that's the best way they can play, then let them play that way. If it's within the rules of the game, then it's up to you how you play.

What's been the most important ingredient in your achieving success?

I was really lucky to have the talent that I had, because when I was young, I never actually wanted to be a footballer and if you don't want to be something, normally you will be left by the wayside. I was also lucky that circumstances forced me back into football. If I look back, I was never as competitive at football than I was at everything else. I was more competitive at golf, squash – almost anything other than football. I don't know what it was about me playing football. Obviously it's indoctrinated in Liverpool that you've got to win, and I think that drags you up to that level of competitiveness. What it comes down to, as far as football was concerned, I could always take it or leave it. Who knows but, if that hadn't been the case and my first love had been football, I think I might have been better at it.

What would you do differently if you had your time again?

I suppose I would have been fitter. Nowadays the attitude towards fitness and diet is so much better than it was when I was playing. I did look after myself well and when I got to 30, I was resting up four or five times a week. I stopped going out very much and I cut down on drinking.

What's the hardest part of being a television pundit?

I am always trying to keep it fresh, trying to come up with different angles, different things that you haven't come up with in the 18 years I have been doing it. It's really difficult. The pitch is the same size, it's 11 players against 11 players. One good thing about the Premiership is that there are so many good players coming in, that's what keeps it fresh. You can talk about tactics only for so long. If you've been doing it for as long as I have, you realise it's always the same tactics, the same style of play, the way people play, but fortunately, the faces are different.

What one-line sentence would you give to anybody aspiring to be the best they could be?

It's something I never did myself, but I would say: always listen to advice. I know that sounds rather hypocritical but I would say listen to advice, and listen to experience.

Which sportsman or sportswoman from another sport do you admire the most and why?

Obviously, Tiger Woods is the one that sticks out. Not only because he's exciting and he's brought different people into golf, but just because of the mindset. His record is unbelievable; a winner in so many golf tournaments in the States and in Majors. He's just driven. He's got everything: he's exciting to watch, he's got the drive from within, he's got this ability to produce the goods under pressure.

From the world of football, I'd always say Joe Fagan is the man I admired the most. If you ever had a problem, you'd go to Joe. I was never one to seek advice, but Joe would come and have a word in your ear at the right time and you'd listen to him. He was a great, great man.

KARL MORRIS SUMMARY

A Swedish psychologist by the name of Anders Ericsson has spent the best part of the last twenty years studying the concept of 'talent'. How and why someone is so good at what they do.

Is it just handed down by the gods or is it something that can be developed? From Mozart to Bill Gates to Tiger Woods, it seems that Ericsson's life-work can be summed up by the number 10,000!

Somewhat controversially, Ericsson proposes that to 'become' a genius takes 10,000 hours of practice. Talent isn't just a question of random selection, it is a result of a deep absorption in an activity which you LOVE to do. Alan Hansen's description of his upbringing would certainly resonate with Anders Ericsson.

"I used to come back from school at 4 o'clock, and immediately start kicking the ball against that wall. And doing it non-stop for hours and hours, by myself – left foot, right foot, left foot, right foot."

This is someone who put the time in and the effort to become a genius on the football field. No short-cuts; time served in doing something that he loved to do. It is also fascinating to hear Alan being so open and honest about how he felt before a game or indeed how he feels even now, just before he goes on to *Match of the Day*. The cause of all these feelings of anxiety can be summed up in one word: DOUBT. It is part of the make-up of us all that we, to a greater or lesser degree, have some element of doubt inside us.

If this is you, and you suffer with an extreme element of doubt then let Alan Hansen be an example to you that you CAN achieve greatness in spite of some of these feelings. If you have prepared, if you have looked at what you need to do to be your best, you can be outstanding. For Alan, as soon as he stepped on the pitch or as soon as the cameras start to roll, then he is fine.

I believe the knowledge is now available, through improvements in understanding how the brain works, so that these pre-match feelings can be channelled and reduced. You may not totally eliminate your 'nerves', but you can learn to train your brain just as you would learn to train your body.

The insights into the Liverpool boot room also give us an absolute nugget of priceless information. Having won the European Cup but being told by the coach Joe Fagan they should improve the next year - by winning the all-important League Championship - shows an essential element to truly great success: that of avoiding complacency at all cost. Celebrate your victory yes; wallow in it, never.

DAMON HILL, OBE

Damon Graham Devereux Hill OBE was born on 17th September 1960, in Hampstead, London and is a retired British racing-driver. He was educated at Haberdashers' Aske's Boys' School in Elstree, Hertfordshire.

In 1994, he was voted BBC Sports Personality of the Year, after losing out to Michael Schumacher for the Formula One Championship in the most bitter of circumstances. He won this BBC award for a second time in 1996 when he became the 1996 Formula One world champion, thereby following in the footsteps of his father, the late Graham Hill, a two-time world champion. He is the only son of a world champion to have achieved this feat.

He retired from motor racing after the 1999 season and has since launched several businesses, as well as making appearances playing the guitar with celebrity bands. In 2006, he became President of the British Racing Drivers' Club, succeeding Sir Jackie Stewart.

QUESTIONS

What's your first memory of motor racing?

It's almost impossible to give you an answer to that. When you consider that Stirling Moss came to my christening, and that I was basically looked after in the paddock from birth, it is almost impossible to give you a precise date. I am not someone who came to the sport from the outside. I was on the inside looking out. You might as well ask me what my first memory was of another life outside motor-racing – in which case I'd probably say going to prep school or something like that.

Your father Graham was a two-time world champion. What do you remember of his career?

Now at this point, I remember an awful lot. I was very aware of him when I was growing up. I knew my Dad, I knew he did this as a job, and I thought it was perfectly normal and everything else was abnormal. I can remember watching him, when I was about 10, winning the International Trophy Race at Silverstone, but I was more interested in the result of the FA Cup final. I saw him win the Monaco Grand Prix on television in 1969. That was certainly an impression because it was on television. In those days, motor racing wasn't shown on television regularly. I remember playing with a friend in the garden and my Mum called me in to watch Daddy win the Monaco Grand Prix. I thought, "Oh God, must I?" But I went and saw it and thought "Oh, that's my Dad on television. Wow." He won the Monaco Grand Prix and I went back to playing in the garden.

For a 15-year-old at the time of his tragic death in 1975, just how difficult a period was this?

Being such a large personality and really dominating the scene wherever he went, his death left a big hole. It was a real case of having to get some bearings really, and that's quite difficult. You're left with his legacy, which was his attitude to life I suppose, as a guide. My father thought every day was a party. He thought every day was a blessing and a great opportunity. He was completely full-on in his life, so to say his life was cut short, he'd probably say he actually packed a lot in. Some people don't care about the length of their life, which others might view as reckless. Some people would regard anyone being a racing-driver as being reckless. What I would say about people of his era - and I won't just single out my Dad here - is that they were the post-war generation and their lives were set against the experiences of the Second World War. To them, every day that you weren't at war was a bonus. Getting in a racing-car was relatively safe, next to getting into a fighter or a tank, doing what those people around you were doing at the time, who were being blitzed. It's all a question of degree. My Mum's house at school was split into an A group and a B group, by alphabet. She was in the morning group and when they came out, the afternoon lot went in and that half of the class got bombed and was wiped out. My Mum was in the half that happened to survive. My Dad and my Mum went through that experience. And their parents had been through that, and the First World War, plus the Great Depression. You have to put their lives in the context of that history. Nowadays, it is frowned upon massively to live the life my father did; it was a rock-and-roll attitude to life, which is now seen as being almost foolhardy.

Did you make a commitment to yourself after his death to try everything within your power to follow in your father's footsteps and aim to become world-champion yourself?

No, I didn't know what I wanted to do. I just wanted to be successful in whatever I did. So I dabbled with the usual things, I had some friends who were into music, and I mentally toyed with the idea of being in a band and I played with some friends, but I wasn't very good. I understood motor-racing of course, but my thing was bike-racing. I loved bikes; I loved being on a bike. So I just did that. That's what I wanted to do, I wanted to race bikes, and I absolutely loved the motorbike Grand Prix. I had posters on my wall of Agostini, Barry Sheene and Freddie Spencer. They were my role models. I read bike magazines. I loved the fact that it was anti-establishment. That was my alternative lifestyle if you like, being into bikes.

You were 23 when you first entered professional motorsports. How did you get there?

After I left school, I did any job just to get cash. I got cash to buy some bikes and I managed to get some support. I was doing everything on my own and doing everything wrong. When I was young, I just didn't trust anyone to help me, I did it all myself. After a while, I finally found my feet and started winning races. Interestingly, it wasn't until I got to the point where I was winning that people wanted to help me. Up until that point, it had been a struggle. But as soon as I started winning on bikes, there was interest in me. John Webb, the Brands Hatch supremo, helped me get a car-race and then I started looking for sponsorship and, because I had won something, people started believing in me and I managed to get some backing for car-racing. So I did half a season in 1984/85, before I had my first ever full season. I was 24 and I had managed to bag a few quid to live on. I regard that as being my first professional year of being a racing-driver, although it was subsistence living, I was happy with that. I was doing something which went towards making me successful.

Aged 26, and following the death of your team-mate Bertrand Fabi, you borrowed £100,000 to get you into the British Formula 3 Championship. You said that you were frightened of letting things slip and ending up aged 60 having achieved nothing. Was this fear of failure the driving force behind you?

For me, it wasn't a fear of failure, more a fear of not having done something. I had read about Niki Lauda who had borrowed some money to go racing and the rationale he used was: in order to do this, I have to believe that I am going to be successful. He believed it was OK to borrow the money, because he believed he was going to be in a position to pay it back. If you don't believe you are going to be successful, you won't be. And I thought that was an amazing way of looking at it - you can't argue with that. If you don't think you are going to win, then don't do it. There are those who believe that life is sacred and that you must preserve it at all costs. They will sit under a tree cross-legged and meditate, and that's life to them. The other attitude – like my Dad's - is you've got it, so spend it and pack in as

much as you can. All humans need experiences; experiences make us. To me, it is no good just sitting there and conjecturing, you have to go out there and try your hand at something and find out whether your beliefs and theories about life and yourself hold up. So you put yourself in those situations, and you might realise that you're not quite the all-singing, all-dancing person you thought you were. Or you say to yourself, I don't want to back down at this point and I'm going to put myself through this test. You can't do that if you don't do anything. Your body is a tool for going through life. You can keep it in the tool-box or you can take it out and use it. It's going to get worn out anyway, so you might as well use it - that's life.

Aged 31, you were a test driver for Williams, whilst still driving in the F3000 Championship. Was it a case of being patient and waiting for your moment to arrive?

It's like going to the front in a Formula One race - there are people at the front, some of them drop out and eventually you move up the queue. I started at the back but, as long as I had my bum in a seat and was going round racetracks, then I knew that there was a chance that a front-running opportunity would come up. But if you are not in the frame, then you have no chance. So it was a case of just keeping my hand on the steering-wheel and waiting.

Midway through the following season (1993), you got your break with Brabham. How did it feel to finally be behind the wheel in a Formula One race?

Signing for Brabham was really something. Some managers might have advised against it, because everyone wants to be in the best car. But I always had to struggle, and my attitude was, even if I'm in the worst car, I will show you what I can do with it. Being behind the wheel in my first F1 race was fun. I never thought I would get that far, and there I was, still in the hunt, still in the game, and being given another chance. So, I just gave it my best shot every time and saw what happened.

The next season, following Nigel Mansell's departure from Williams, you were promoted to race alongside triple world champion Alain Prost. How much did you learn from him at this time?

I was a big Alain Prost fan. He was such a stylish driver. He had such sublime talent and speed. He was just great. I was very humbled and honoured to be in the team with him. But, although I admired him and looked up to him, of course another part of you thinks, if I can beat him, that would be great. So I tried to beat him. I was conscious that this was the tail-end of his career, not the beginning, and this was my first attempt and I was on the up – and I was hungry. I learnt a little from Alain, but he tended to keep his cards close to his chest. He was very charming but such an experienced competitor, so why would he give me advice and help? I was trying to beat him, so I completely respect that. It's not his job to help me.

In your 19th Formula One race, you won the Hungarian Grand Prix and then followed this up with back-to-back wins in Belgium and Italy. Just how good was it to win your first race?

It was good, but to be honest, I didn't know whether I deserved it. It all unfolded in front of me and I just happened to be in front at the end. I felt like I had driven well, but I wanted to win a race where there were no questions about it. For me, it was about finding out myself how good I was. Sport is a very difficult area in which to quantify exactly how good you are. You are only as good as the competition you are up against. And if those people are rated as being the best, that is the target. Being with Prost was a good test for me. I just wanted to know how I measured against the best guys. It was great to have broken through and got a Grand Prix win because that's like climbing Everest, having been at base camp beforehand: it's a long way to the summit.

Of your 22 Formula One wins, was winning the British Grand Prix in 1994 the highlight?

At the time, I didn't quite know how to place it in the scheme of things, because they black-flagged Michael Schumacher, so I won it but I wanted to win a race where I drove absolutely to the very best, where I would know exactly where I stood. It was great from the point of view of being a British driver at the British Grand Prix. It was a very satisfying experience. I had met all the hopes and dreams of the fans, but I was still looking for that moment when you perform absolutely at the very top of your ability.

In the final race of the 1994 season you were one point behind Michael Schumacher in the driver's championship. He became world champion for the first time by making sure that you did not pass him, with both of you out of the race following a collision. How often do you think about that moment and what are your feelings about it?

For me it was a case of it being just another experience. The previous race in Suzuka, Japan, was a very important experience for me because I had satisfied myself that I could race and challenge the very best drivers out there. At the time, it wasn't known exactly how good Michael was. I knew that he was someone who was formidable and difficult to beat. I thought there were more levels I would have to go through in order to be able to compete against him. The Suzuka race confirmed to me that I could just about beat him, if I really tried. He was good and he was unbelievably difficult to beat. I counted this race as a victory though, because he crashed. That's why what happened, happened. After that, it's down to what the stewards and the sporting authorities decide.

Two years later, in 1996, you won the World Championship - and a second BBC Sports Personality of the Year. Of all the things required to get you to this landmark, what was the single most important ingredient?

I was overwhelmed by it actually. I rose to various challenges which is probably why I got recognised. I had been a test-driver for Nigel Mansell, was a team-mate with Alain Prost, then team-mates to Ayrton Senna, so aged 33, I had got myself in the state of mind where I thought it was great to be racing against these guys, but I hadn't imagined myself being the main contender for the Championship. But I think I rose to that challenge, took on that burden and seized the opportunity. Looking back now, I give myself more of a pat on the back than I did at the time, because then I just thought I was doing the best I could. I just wanted to live up to the challenge. You get a challenge and you want to do the best you can in that situation. That's how we progress in life. That's what defines us.

Did you have a set routine for mentally preparing before each race?

I always made sure I was at the track on time so I didn't miss anything. As a racer, you develop your own system of dealing with things. When I was training, I had a heart-rate monitor on to make sure my heart-rate was at a certain level. If I started to think about the race, my heart-rate would go up. So you learn how to control your body through your mind and you save all your energy for the race. You develop an inner space which you have to keep for yourself before the race. Whatever else is going on around you is just froth. So you put on metaphorical blinkers and you deal with things that are extraneous with the amount of energy you need and then you focus on the things that really matter. The process of focusing on the details that are pertinent is a mental discipline - a psyching-up. You make sure you know exactly where you are and what you need to know. That was my mental preparation. It's not that complicated after that; you just go as fast as you can!

Do you think you can control your mind?

I think it is possible to control your mind, definitely, but I think it's very easy to be distracted. It is part of any competitor's necessary skill-set to be able to focus on what they are there to do and be absolutely in the right zone - not behind, not ahead.

What do you feel is your most destructive emotion and how do you deal with it?

I don't like losing. If you can imagine a 4-year-old boy who is having a tantrum, because he's not got what he wants, there's a little bit of that in me. Sometimes you have nowhere to go, because it's either your fault, or what you wanted has been denied you. That's not what you want so you have a destructive moment. But then inevitably you have to come to terms with reality. I think if I didn't have that energy in me then I would not try so hard to win. I've tried to work out whether it's a fear of losing or just wanting to win - and I don't think you can separate the two. It's the carrot and the stick. Everyone needs a bit of carrot and a bit of stick. I think it's better to have more carrot, but sometimes you have to give yourself a bit of stick as well.

What did you do whenever you felt nervous?

I was always more nervous of the politics of F1 than I ever was driving a car. The more nerve-racking thing was not getting a drive. So when you have a car, you are not nervous, because you know you are doing something you know you can do. The word 'nervous' does not compute for me. You simply can't be nervous. If it's raining hard, you must be committed to it. You can't be nervous; you have made a decision and there is no turning back. In pre-qualifying, when you know you have to perform to your maximum for one lap, nerves have negative connotations. You might have doubts or you may be intimidated by what you are about to do, but you can always stop. Any nerves are more to do with worrying about not being able to do your best; will you be able to perform to the level of the best you can? I was never worried about the danger element of racing as you can always take the necessary precautions. Once you are in the car, you already know what you are going to do. In really torrential conditions, your mind might start to wonder whether they should stop the race, but you can always slow down. You can get overtaken and you can always stop.

What one-line sentence would you give to anybody aspiring to be the best they could be?

You must look at life as a discovery about yourself. As a species, we have way more capability than we believe ourselves to have. It's good to take on challenges, because you learn from them and then you grow from them.

Inside and outside of F1, which sportsman or sportswoman do you admire the most and why?

If I was forced to pick one from Formula One, I'd have to pick my Dad. He epitomised the spirit that you can do it if you want to. He always said nothing is impossible. He was someone who had a way of dealing with things. He didn't think that, because he was a racing-driver, he was somehow special. For him, it was a skill, but not a licence.

Outside of F1, there was something about Muhammad Ali. He's a hero, the people's hero. Mind you, Joe Frazier would probably say something different!

KARL MORRIS SUMMARY

Even though, from my own background as a golfer, I have little knowledge of motorsport, I have to say that I found Damon Hill's words absolutely hypnotic. Here is a man who has, on so many levels, achieved tremendous feats, not least of which is that he followed in the footsteps of a truly outstandingly successful father and became a success in his own right in the same field. This is a VERY rare accomplishment. It is clear, though, that Graham Hill left a legacy to his son. Not least was his zest for life, his willingness to get the best out of every day, to seize the moment and the opportunity.

In a way, it may well be that we have all grown up in a period of time which has allowed us to be complacent and not to recognise the need to make the most of our very limited time. It is a cutting insight when Damon talks about experience and the need to get out and 'feel' life: to put yourself on the line, to see what you are capable of, to be able to deal with failure and setback, and to dare to risk and believe. Are we in danger these days of overprotecting ourselves from the possibility of failure? I am not talking about putting your life at risk in a physical sense, but being brave enough to put our sense of self at risk by taking on a challenge with all of the consequences that entails. I am not really a believer in 'positive thinking' as such, but I am TOTALLY in favour of positive DOING.

Backed by the inspirational words of Niki Lauda, who felt that borrowing some money to back yourself was a great formula for belief, Damon Hill took out a loan to give himself the chance to compete in Formula One. He felt that he didn't want to get to the age of 60 having achieved nothing. This is an ACTION of self-belief, not just a statement or a thought. Whilst all things begin with thought, your own future is only going to be determined by your actions. Maybe it is the ultra-dangerous world of motor-racing which clarifies the mind and reinforces that time is not in limitless supply.

I love Damon's take on nerves: "You CAN'T be nervous". You are committed to what you are doing. He is so right. To be successful, we must fly in the face of our uneasy sensations and commit to a course of action. It is facing these uneasy feelings head-on and overcoming them that is at the heart of mental TOUGHNESS.

Damon Hill epitomises this and I urge all of you wanting to change the circumstances of your current life to read this chapter more than once.

GEORGINA HULME

Georgina Hulme was born on 28th November, 1976. Born with Down's Syndrome, the doctor told her parents, Barry and Joan, that she would be "not much more than a cabbage who will string one or two words together". She was educated at Springfield Special School in Crewe, and Russett Special School in Northwich. She then went to Weaverham Wallerscote Primary School and Rudheath High School in Northwich.

With the support of her parents and siblings, Georgina became a talented athlete. She has been involved in Special Olympics since 1984. In this time, she has won the hearts of everyone she has been in contact with, not to mention the many medals from her career as a gymnast. In 1995, Georgina went to college and completed a 3-year course in "Learning for Life" and followed this by doing a 2-year course in catering, gaining NVQ Level 1 in general catering skills and NVQ Level 2 in fast food. She now works as an assistant chef at the Mill Pool restaurant in Little Budworth, Cheshire.

Having retired from gymnastics in 1995, she switched her attentions to swimming, where she has found further success, not only for herself, but in coaching other younger athletes from the Penguins Special Olympics swimming club. In 2004, she was appointed as an Ambassador for Special Olympics GB, being the first athlete to take on this role for the charity. Georgina has spoken at various high-profile public engagements, as well as appearing on *Ready Steady Cook* with England goalkeeper David James. She has met the Kennedy family in America, as well as appearing on American Coast-to-Coast television.

QUESTIONS

When did you first come into contact with Special Olympics?

I first started with Special Olympics in 1983. Aged 7, I started gymnastics whilst I was at a special school in Northwich, and this was good because I was a very energetic young girl and I used to go all over the place – onto climbing frames etc. So finding gymnastics was good for getting rid of that energy.

What were your first major games and what do you remember of them?

It was the European games in Dublin in 1985. I did the floor routine and the vault. It was great as I got to meet lots of people. I ended up doing pretty well. I remember I was so small, like a tiny version of Nadia Comaneci, and I won two silver medals, which I was very happy with.

You met the late Eunice Kennedy Shriver at these games. The sister of President John F Kennedy, she was the founder of the Special Olympics movement in 1968, believing that sport would give confidence and new hope to people with learning disabilities. To what degree did these games in Dublin give you new confidence?

Meeting Eunice Shriver and the Kennedy family for the first time in Dublin was lovely. I think I opened up their hearts. To this day, she is always in my heart and her passing away was a great loss to me. She told me to be brave in my sport. Competing in these games made me feel really good. When I was very young, I couldn't sit still. Gymnastics built up my body strength. It gave me confidence, and I was able to look people in the eye. It also helped me to concentrate and having to concentrate on the gymnastics floor helped me to concentrate in other areas of my life.

During the World Games in South Bend, Indiana, you met the rest of the Kennedy family and you appeared on a Coast-to-Coast TV show. This must have been a really exciting time for you?

I was shocked because I didn't know that I was going on Coast-to-Coast television in America. I did my full floor-routine for television and Mary Lou Retton [American gymnast] came over with the microphone afterwards and gave me a perfect 10! Eunice Shriver was there too, and she came over and gave me a big hug.

Tell me about your friendship with Michael Crawford.

I met Michael in Manchester at the Copley Sports Centre. I was performing in a display team and Michael picked me up on his shoulders and said that he would show me the way. He told me that I was the Barnum babe! Michael is a qualified gymnastics coach and he had come along to watch. It was at the time that he had his show *Barnum* in Manchester. He was my best friend for a while and he sent me some very nice letters.

You became good friends with the late Helen Rollason who gave Special Olympics a big plug with the BBC. What do you remember of the 1989 Sports Personality of the Year awards?

I won my first gymnastics title at the Leicester Games in 1989 and Helen came along to those games to report on the event. I didn't know that I was on *Grandstand* [on the BBC]. After that, she spoke with her BBC colleagues and said she wanted to put me forward for the Sports Personality of the Year award in 1989, which she did. I was nominated for this award and I ended up getting more votes than Nigel Mansell! Steve Davis came third and was very disappointed and ended up leaving the studio. Nick Faldo won it and Frank Bruno was second. Frank told me to come over and pose for the photo in third place as Steve had gone! It was a very special evening for me. I would love to do that again some time. I met a lot of people who were so friendly and it was great to see so many people.

The motto for Special Olympics is "Let me win. But if I cannot win, let me be brave in the attempt." How important is it to have a desire to win and be the best one can be?

All of the Special Olympics athletes get the opportunity to be brave in their sports, their career and their achievements. Everyone can try to do their best, if they get fit. For people with a disability like me, you get an opportunity to win at the games, to be brave at the games. Eunice used to say that it is an honour to compete and that if you want to win, you can win. If you keep that message in your heart, you can win. I used to watch a film about Nadia Comaneci. When she broke the record with a perfect 10 on the bars, I loved it. Since then, I always followed her footsteps. She was one of my heroes. I also got to meet Daniela Silivas, when the Romanian team visited the Copley Centre.

What has been your proudest moment since first joining Special Olympics in 1984?

I feel proud of all moments in the past; seeing people with learning disabilities compete makes me feel proud. I would really like to follow in Eunice's footsteps and carry on the message that she started. I would love to open a Special Olympics games in the future. That's why I am so proud to be an ambassador for the organisation. Through my competing and coaching, I feel a real responsibility for the athletes. I am the athletes' contact person, their director, so I am there for them. They can write to me or talk to me, about whatever issue they may have, and I will try to help them.

Of all the medals you have won in your career, which one is the most important to you?

I was the first person in this country with a learning disability to be awarded the Master Gymnast's medal, which was awarded to me by British Gymnastics. I was awarded this medal in 1991.

What might life have been like for you without Special Olympics?

I think that it would have been difficult. It is far better for me to be in Special Olympics. The organisation has really done a lot for me.

What does Special Olympics give to its people?

The biggest thing that the organisation gives to people is courage. You have to fight. In order to achieve, you have to make sure you are ready to compete.

What do you enjoy more? Competing or coaching?

I coach swimming every Thursday and every Sunday. I do this as a volunteer and the council awards points for this work. If you get to 100 points, you get a t-shirt and if you get to 200 points, you get a fleece, which is what I have. I like to do both, compete and coach.

You are now on the board of Special Olympics GB. How much do you enjoy being the representative for all athletes in England, Scotland and Wales?

I was pleased and shocked when I found out that I had been asked to take on this role. I have done this role since 2005 and it is a great honour for me.

There are approximately 1.2 million people in Great Britain with a learning disability. What advice would you offer to anyone with a learning disability who is interested in getting into sport?

For anyone with a disability, whether physical or learning, my advice would be to find a sport to compete in. You should make sure that the sport is right for you and that you are comfortable competing in it. After that, you should practise and train – and work hard. Some of our athletes can't talk, so we have helpers who can assist them. I just want people to try a sport out and then keep doing it. If anyone with a learning disability [with an IQ of 75 or under] wants to be involved in Special Olympics, they should pick up the phone and call the Special Olympics Head Office in London. They can then find out what group is nearest to them.

Special Olympics GB continues to get no support from either the Government or the National Lottery. Just how important is it to continue to raise funds on a year-by-year basis?

It is so important to get money; this gives athletes the chance to compete. When we meet for board-meetings, we discuss what events are next, and what needs to happen – just like we did for the 2009 games in Leicester. The next world games are in Athens in 2011. This all needs money. We can all play a part in fundraising. Be it a tombola or a disco, all the athletes can try and raise money for the charity. Without this money, there would be no games. It would be great to have the Government commit some funds for Special Olympics. At the summer games in Leicester 2009, I met Gordon Brown and his wife Sarah again. I had met them before at 10 Downing Street, at a drinks reception for Special Olympics, before our Grand Gala for the 30th anniversary. When I walked down the stairs at Number 10, I remember thinking crikey, this is a nice house. With the great work that is being done by everyone at Special Olympics, including the Chairman, Lawrie McMenemy, we would like to think that we may get some government support in the future.

You have been lucky to meet several members of the Royal family?

Yes, I met the Queen in Norfolk when she opened a leisure-centre. I met Princess Diana twice and I have also met Prince Charles and Princess Anne. Our gymnastics team put on a display for Prince Charles at an event in London.

What do you hope this book will achieve for Special Olympics GB?

I hope that this book raises some much-needed money for our charity. I also hope that the book raises the profile of our organisation. If the book can spread the word and get people to understand what Special Olympics is, then all the better.

What's been the most important ingredient in your achieving success?

I have wanted to win all the time. Once I saw Nadia Comaneci win, I wanted to do the same.

Which sportsman or sportswoman from another sport do you admire the most and why?

Nadia Comaneci. She kept on winning and wanted to be the best. She fought to win and I love that. She was hungry for success.

KARL MORRIS SUMMARY

Life is all about difference and being able to understand. We all have tastes and opinions which will never be uniform in nature. Yet, I must admit I find it hard personally to understand someone who says, "I don't like sport."

One of the revealing aspects of working on this book has been the underlying message of the huge role that sport plays in so many lives. It would be very easy to question the point of chasing a ball round a field or throwing something or running after someone. But this misses the point entirely.

Sport has given so many of us structure, experience, camaraderie, bravery, discipline - the list goes on and on. In this particular chapter, about Special Olympics athlete Georgina Hulme, it is abundantly clear that here is someone who has been presented with a challenge in life, but who has responded magnificently through the medium of sport. Her incredibly rich experience of life has been shaped by the possibilities provided by sport.

I have been fortunate to work with many Special Olympic athletes and have witnessed the joy being absorbed in sport has brought to them all. I think it is imperative we all keep up our efforts in bringing sport to future generations. If we don't, it will be our loss as well as theirs.

Make no mistake though, when you get the opportunity to work with or assist Special Olympics athletes, do not underestimate how much they, as athletes with learning disabilities, desire to win and perform at their very best. It is so apparent reading Georgina's account of competing as a gymnast and a swimmer that she went out to win and be the best she could be. Just as in mainstream sport, you can see this winning spirit was enhanced by exactly the same kind of protocols as the rest of the stars in this book. As with many others, she has been hugely influenced by supportive parents and coaches. Georgina realised she needed to improve her levels of concentration and did so with dedicated application.

She had her imagination fired by the brilliance of Nadia Comaneci. As Georgina states: "She kept on winning and wanted to be the best. She fought to win and I love that. She was hungry for success."

We all need role-models. We all need people we can look up to and be inspired by as we face our own individual challenges in life. Just as Georgina Hulme was inspired by the great Romanian gymnast, Nadia Comaneci, she should be very proud of herself as I am sure when reading her extraordinary story of success by overcoming adversity, you too will be inspired to be the best you can be.

DAVID JAMES

David Benjamin James was born on 1ˢᵗ August 1970 in Welwyn Garden City, Hertfordshire. He was educated at The Ryde School in Hatfield and Sir Frederic Osborn School in Welwyn Garden City. He is a goalkeeper who currently plays for English football club Portsmouth and the England national team.

On 14 February 2009, he passed Gary Speed's all-time Premier League record, making his 536th appearance. He gained a Football League Cup winner's medal with Liverpool in 1995, and an FA Cup winner's medal with Portsmouth in 2008, as well as FA Cup runners-up medals with Liverpool in 1996 and with Aston Villa in 2000.

James made his England debut in 1997 and is currently Fabio Capello's number-one goalkeeper. Fitness permitting, he will be a key member of the England squad at the 2010 World Cup in South Africa.

He is also an ambassador for Special Olympics Great Britain.

QUESTIONS

Who introduced you to the game?

I only started to understand football when I was 9 or 10 years old. Football didn't play much of a role in my life before that. It was at my junior school and there was a Leeds Utd versus Man Utd battle going on in the playground, with everyone in their respective group chanting for their team. I think I was chanting for Leeds as my grandparents came from there. It wasn't until I started playing football at school, as part of games lessons after school, that I started to develop an interest in the game.

Can you remember the first game you watched at a stadium?

I think it was Luton Town versus Hull, but I couldn't be sure. We were taken to the game by Welwyn Pegasus which was the first Sunday team I played for. I didn't have a clue what was going on. My Uncle was a Luton Town fan when he was alive and I remember Lorraine Chase being famous for saying "Luton Airport". So when someone said that I was going to watch Luton, I thought it was an airport! I am still a Luton Town fan myself, of sorts, based on those early experiences at Kenilworth Road.

Why did you choose to be a goalkeeper?

First of all, it was because I couldn't kick a ball and I didn't really understand what football was about. At my second junior school, there was a games lesson going on and I was stuck in the middle of the field. The lad in goal wasn't doing much so I thought I'd try and do better and that was it. I just took to it. It's the age-old thing: people tell you that you are good at something, so you continue to do it.

How good did you think you were as a youngster?

I didn't think I was good at all; it was based on other people's opinions. I was just doing what my mates were doing. They lived and breathed football. One lad I was at school with, Daniel Novelli, his Mum was secretary of the team and she asked me how old I was. I was the same age as Dan but was a school-year above him, but being born on August 1st meant that I could play football for the year below, so I ended up going to training with Dan. That's how I got involved with the lads.

When were you spotted by a professional club?

When I was 12 or 13, I went to Tottenham for a year. I really can't remember all of the details of how that happened; it's still a bit of a mystery. I played school football, Sunday football, County football. When I played a game for Tottenham against Watford, we got beaten 6-2 and a lad called Rod Thomas scored five goals. I thought my football career was over but Watford asked me and a friend to go and join them, which I did at the age of 13.

Did you have any thoughts of not making it in football?

Yes. I really didn't know that I wanted to make it in the first place when I was about 15. I went along and played the games but, at the same time, I was heavily involved in athletics. I had a troubled school life. I wasn't a really bad egg, but I was a little disruptive and I just didn't have any focus at school, although I was told that I was pretty good at athletics, particularly the high jump. I didn't do anything amazing but apparently I had a lot of raw talent which could have been nurtured and, at the age of 15, I was given the opportunity to either pursue a career in athletics or football. For the first and only time in my life, I was driven by money because there was no money in athletics and there was £24.50 a week in football on the Youth Training Scheme (YTS) at Watford, as well as digs. That was what swayed it.

When was it clear that you were going to make it professionally?

I don't think it was ever clear. I meet kids all the time who have aspirations and dreams of being a footballer. But I never had that. I did things only because I was good at them. When I started my career, there was a lot of violence in football, crowd trouble, hooliganism and, even then, I couldn't see a future in football because I didn't understand how the game worked and what it meant to people socially. So, becoming a footballer was not a childhood dream of mine. I got my apprenticeship, did two years, considered myself rather fortunate to have a third year in the youth team, and we won the Youth Cup which was good. I was taken on as a professional, signing a three-year deal with Watford. I had a year in the reserves where I was awful. I worked under a lot of people: Graham Taylor looked after the Youth Team at the time, then Dave Bassett took over for a bit, then Steve Harrison, who signed me as a professional, then there was Colin Lee, followed by Steve Perryman. My year in the reserve team was my worst ever. I genuinely thought my career was over as I hadn't really thought about any alternative plan. The following season though, I got into the first team at Watford. I went in to see the manager after a few games and asked him what was happening with my contract, as I wanted to know how my long-term future looked, and he told me that when I'd played 10 games, he'd sit down with me and talk about it. But he then got the sack and he told me not to sign another contract as there were lots of other clubs interested in me. At this point football became a bit more real for me.

Who was the biggest single influence in helping you get there?

There isn't just one; there are many. Had Daniel's Mum not taken the five minutes to look through the rules, then I wouldn't have joined his team. I could easily have got interested in something else. Then there was Tom Whalley, who was a Youth Team coach at Watford and was my father-figure in football. He was awesome. Then there was my Nan who used to take me down to training at Woodside in Watford, where she would sit and learn her musical scores (she was a pianist at the local church) and then take me home again, as my Mum didn't drive. Had it not been for Nan doing that, anything could have happened. There are so many different influences.

Was there a seminal day in your career which you would pick out as being the most important for you?

That was my debut. We lost 2-1 against Millwall at Vicarage Road. The second goal wasn't a goal; it was a Malcolm Allen header which I saved but, for some reason, the linesman gave the goal. I was so disappointed coming off the field having lost and I wondered whether I was going to get bombed out - but I didn't.

Do you have a set routine for mentally preparing before each game?

I do now, yes. I have my own sports psychologist, Keith Power, who I have been using for nearly eight years now, since my time at Aston Villa. Before I started working with Keith, I would be in a sort of zone for 48 hours, thinking am I doing the right thing here, am I doing the right thing there? Not doing this, not doing that – which was mad really. What we do now is work on the imagery stuff. Before the game, I go in the shower and for 20 minutes I go through all the shots and crosses in my mind. I have now got to the point where it is not about what I do on the day of the game, it is all about what I do before the game. My weekly plan and preparation leading up to the game will influence how I play, not what I do in the shower for 20 minutes before the game, as that is just the fine-tuning. I like to keep my mind calm. After the shower, I get a little more physical in the changing-room, where I go through various body-motions and then banging the ball against the wall, all of which is heightening the senses. Some people like to get really hyped-up which makes them play better, but for me the preparation starts a week beforehand. Before kick-off, I just get mentally and physically warmed up and tuned in, and then I am ready to go. The old-fashioned mentality was that you did everything on a Friday, then on the Saturday, you'd get warmed up and go out onto the park. When I played for Liverpool, we always knew we were going to be better than most teams. Most of the time, everything would seem right. But that was the difficulty - we used to go out and do warm-ups for an hour before a game. Then one day at Anfield, the groundsman said to me that my warm-up was too much. I was literally coming off in a pool of sweat which was hardly the right preparation for the match. It's little things like that - the work-to-performance ratio wasn't quite right.

Did you stumble across sports psychology at Aston Villa?

Keith Power was brought in for the season we got to the FA Cup Final. Afterwards, he said he was looking to do some one-to-one sessions and asked if I was interested, and I said I was, definitely. I saw the immediate benefit of this relationship with Keith. The fact that I am still playing now shows you what it has done for me. Of course you could argue that physiology would have something to do with my longevity but the reality is that without the mental side of the game it doesn't matter how good you are physically, you are always going to suffer and if you continue to suffer, then people don't want you. I am back in the national side as a result of my performances – and Keith has played a big part in that.

What percentage weighting would you give to the physical versus mental side of being a goalkeeper?

These are two parts of a multi-layered pie. There are physical and contextual aspects to this. The reality is not so much thinking about how I play, it is controlling everything outside in the day-to-day routine. I'm into my fourth season at Portsmouth now and, in the first two seasons, I was travelling to and from Devon, two or three times a week – more than 50,000 miles a year. I had to make sure that I could do that without fatiguing me or impacting on my performance in a negative way. There were times when my head was frying, but by then I was better organised about what I did in the day, and I was also taking a more professional view of my career.

Do you think you can control your mind when you step out onto a football field?

This might sound absolutely mad, but I am in control, yet knowing that there are going to be fluctuations. I can't say that I go out there and know that I am 100% totally positive because that's not true. Even during my preparations, I think bad things, not because I feel down on myself but I have to be aware of the potential of something not going right – but the secret is knowing how you then counteract these thoughts. So yes, on the field, I am in control.

What do you feel is your most destructive emotion and how do you deal with it?

My wife refers to me as an emotionless soul! I've got to a stage, and maybe this isn't happy reading for a fanatic, as they might not fully understand it, but I try to trim off the highs and lows. That's how it works best for me. The loss of emotional control means the loss of objectivity, so you literally go out, you do a job, you're happy if you win and you're happy if you keep a clean sheet, then you get back in the changing-room and are pleased with the performance, and then next game you have to do the same again. And it doesn't matter where you are in the league: bottom, towards the middle or at the top, there's always the next game.

You are a keen student of psychology and have been for some time now. Can you give me some examples of how your understanding of psychology has helped your game?

The self-talk work in training is very important. The imagery work in the shower, that's the match day routine, but during training, if I am on a bike in the gym, I will do a bit of imagery work or whenever I can fit it in. Self-talking is another thing. You don't walk off the pitch and think, great, I am the best in the world because you can guarantee that there's something around the corner which is not quite so good that will disappoint you. But if something goes badly, you say, OK, let's do it again, let's work at it and understand why it went badly. This is not necessarily a verbal or audible thing. A lot of it is self-talk in your head. Quite literally, you are talking to your mind.

Robert Enke, the Hannover 96 and German goalkeeper, committed suicide recently and his death was a real shock to the football world. His father Dirk is a sports psychologist, but was unable to treat Robert given their relationship. Dirk talks about Robert's struggle to keep up with his ambition and how he had a constant fear of failure. Robert was also frightened to talk about his depression for fear of ruining his career. Do you think Robert's sad death may lift the lid on what is perceived to be a taboo subject?

I have only heard snippets about this, so I don't know the full extent which his depression had got to and what he had tried to do to cure it. Is it a neglected subject for footballers? I've done some work for testicular cancer charities which is also an area that, as you say, is taboo. Because there is a campaign out there, the issue has been raised and therefore will save a lot of lives hopefully. Unfortunately, an incident like the Enke suicide might well do some good, although it is difficult to say how much.

There seem to be a lot of goalkeepers both past and present who have to be prepared to play the role of understudy in a squad. When

goalkeepers are not in the first team and have to bide their time, just how difficult is this?

I had a spell like this at Liverpool with Brad Friedel. In my first season at Liverpool, I played 31 games and then I didn't play for eight months. You feel terrible. Initially, you feel bad because you've been dropped. And your natural reaction is to try even harder. But sometimes, it doesn't matter what you do you just do not get a chance. Then you can spiral into thinking you have no hope of getting back. When this happened to me at Liverpool, I was four years into my first-team career and, although I was experienced, I started wondering where this left me, especially at a club the size and magnitude of Liverpool, one of the best in the world. But I realised that I just had to wait for an opportunity. Graeme Souness, the manager, left and Roy Evans came in - and not long after that I got another chance in the first team and then I didn't miss a game for two to three years. At Liverpool, as someone explained to me a few years later, the mechanism was set out by Bill Shankly, which was to get as many players as they could, hammer them all and whoever is left over, they'd be the ones they were looking for. That's how the system worked in my time: hammer, hammer, hammer. And if you didn't manage to get through that, then you were left by the wayside. Fortunately for me, I got another opportunity, but I had ballooned to about 17 stone at one point, which is massive - completely out of shape. But I made a mental decision to work hard and get myself right and see what happened. After doing that, I got back in the first team and then cracked on.

You've played professional football for over 20 years. Looking back, do you think you have got mentally stronger year on year?

Since I left Aston Villa, there has been an increase in my mental strength. But I like to think I am at a happy place in my life now.

Would it be fair to say that the role of a goalkeeper is actually the hardest role in the team from a mental perspective, in that you can go for long periods of time and not be in the game, but then when you are in the game, you are under the closest scrutiny?

You could say that about a forward too of course. If you look at a forward in a game, sometimes they don't get a kick of the ball. You might be the only one up front, you're at Old Trafford, standing on the half-way line, then suddenly the ball comes to you, you have to try and deal with it and then you have to deal with Rio Ferdinand and then whoever else. A forward can have a very difficult experience. Is it tough being a goalkeeper? Well, football is tough; there are no hiding places. I have spoken to players through the years and they will tell you how they feel persecuted by fans or the media, in whatever position they play. It's not exclusive to any one position, they all feel the pressure.

How do you go about dealing with that?

The first time I felt under pressure at Liverpool, I didn't know how to deal with it at all. I spoke to coaches and friends to try to work out what was going wrong and they all said I just needed to get on with it – but this advice, I now realise, was rubbish. And that was when I had my very first introduction to sports psychology. I asked at Liverpool if anyone had heard of sports psychology. Everyone pretty much poo-pooed it – all except for the club doctor, who arranged for me to meet someone. We sat down for two hours at his house; we went through a load of things and he explained how I was seeing things from the wrong viewpoint. I was tending to blame myself for things that were going wrong. He put things in a more understandable order and I left that meeting feeling much better. After that, things picked up. As far as the media is concerned, it is a difficult subject. There is a public perception of you in the media and, at the end of the day, football is entertainment and, just like the top glamour models don't always look their best, it is very difficult. When things are going well for you and people react to you in a positive way, you sometimes just want to say it isn't all great. But then you learn that if you knock yourself down, then other people will also knock you down, and it can be very difficult to pick yourself back up again, as people have a set view of what they see on the television or read in the papers. In the end, you just have to accept that it's all part of the entertainment business.

So you have your own self-defence, self-protection mechanism?

Yes I always have had. I enjoy talking to fans. I don't go looking for them, but if someone stops me and asks me questions, I will talk to them, providing that I have the time. It's not because I want to prove them wrong, or put them right on anything, it is just interesting hearing what people's opinions are; which is essentially what football is, a game of opinions.

So do you read the newspapers after games?

No I don't. I have done in the past, but the trouble is these guys that write that you are rubbish, they've never played the game. At the end of the day, these guys are writing stories for an audience which hasn't played the game either. If Patrick Moore went on the Sky at Night and just talked about technical and scientific things, people would be lost. Most people just want to know how bright it is going to be and what time the comet is going to be in the sky. It's the same with football. If everything was broken down into data and terminology, most fans would be lost I think. They like to pick up the paper and read that one player was crap, another was brilliant – which is a general view. All that said, I understand that the reporter writing the story will have his opinion and that is the way it is – and he is entitled to his opinion.

In a 90-minute game, are you concentrating 100% for the whole of the game, no matter where the ball is on the pitch, or do you allow yourself some down-time if the ball is in the opponents' half for example?

I'm not saying that for every game I play I am 100% focused for 90 minutes, because I am not. There may be a player down injured, for example. This is a moment when you try to have two minutes off, depending on how the game is going of course. Or you may try to have a couple of seconds of humour; maybe a fan in the crowd who's been giving you a bit of stick, but then you have to switch straight back on, once the game resumes. I watch the ball, but you have to make sure you are not over-focused. If your vision becomes too tunnelled, you lose the perspective on the pitch and this can affect your judgement sometimes. You can't be over-intense. People talk about "the zone", which is a very strange place. I don't often get in the zone anymore. When you are in it, it feels so different. To come off the field after having had that experience and you can't remember too much of the game, I think can actually be a bad thing because you can't register, process and learn properly.

In the past, for example, if you made a high-profile error playing for England, how would you deal with the criticism and how easy is it for your confidence to be dented?

Interesting question. The game against Denmark in 2005, when I conceded four goals in a 4-1 defeat, is a good example where I got bombed out. This, I think, was all down to preparation, not the night before but the two or three days' preparation leading up to the game. I was disappointed that I didn't do the right things during the game. If the ball bobbles, everyone gives you stick for the bobble - but it's not your fault. When it is your fault, sometimes it is easier as you know why it isn't right. It's another aspect of control. If it is down to me, I put my hands up, accept it, and then carry on.

How do you see other footballers wasting their potential?

How does anyone waste potential anywhere? Footballers are a cross-section of society, whether the male or female species. You name it, they do it. Football is not unique. This is why football is a great game, and why sport in general is a great thing. The elite - the best - do things right more often than anyone else. I personally think you have to have a condition to get to the top, like some sort of autistic condition, because normal people can't push themselves, either physically or mentally, to the limits it requires. If you look at the list of names in this book, you are talking about people who have been at the top of the tree.

Before each game for England, which pressure is greater, the pressure from the watching world or the pressure you put on yourself to do well?

I honestly haven't felt it. Since I have been back in the England side, under Fabio Capello, I haven't felt it. It's great. We meet up, we train, we play. When you go out to play, you feel ready. There's no feeling that you haven't done this or you haven't done that. We know what we have to do; we go out there and we play. I don't know what Mr Capello does for himself, but he tells people what he thinks.

You recently broke the record for the number of all-time Premier League appearances. What has been the secret behind you achieving this historical landmark?

It would have been more if I hadn't have stayed at West Ham for those six months! Desire has been the key. Even as an apprentice at Watford, I used to look at all the results, all the clean sheets, how many goals had been conceded, and I would work out which goalkeeper had let in the fewest goals. That was my motivation – I wanted to keep more clean sheets than anyone else. And I still want to do this, and I want to break records. There has always been a target or a goal for me to go for. With the Premier League appearances, I break a record every time I go on the field now. In fact, I break two: most goals conceded and most clean sheets. So one way or the other, I always come off the field with two new records! And I still I have the desire to continue doing what I love doing – it's work, but I enjoy the challenge that work gives me. I enjoy the fact that if Wayne Rooney is in front of me and he hits the ball at 100 miles per hour and I stop it, that means my work for the week has been good. If I let it in, it hasn't been. There are always these challenges. That's been the driving-force behind the records. Once you get to a record, then there should be something else to look for. When Dave Beasant saved the first penalty in a Cup Final, (for Wimbledon against Liverpool in 1988), I was gutted. I wasn't even in the first team at Watford, but I wanted to be the first person to save a penalty in a Cup Final. I want to be the one who is achieving and breaking records. I have written off the England record though, as Peter Shilton has 125 caps to my 48, so I might have to leave that one!

Has sports psychology helped you to get a more balanced perspective on your profession?

Yes, definitely. In the past, if I had let a goal in, I used to be an absolute nightmare to be around. If I let a goal in at Liverpool, I wouldn't even talk to people; I'd be in a proper mood, grizzly and moody. If I kept a clean sheet, I was buzzing, but even then I wouldn't be entirely satisfied. And I'd be upset if I didn't have anything to do. I wouldn't wish to go back in time and do anything different, but if I had the sports psychology knowledge then that I have now, I would have been a completely different beast.

Are you therefore advocating that every professional sportsperson should have a sports psychologist?

I view sports psychology in the same way I view dieting and sports science. If you eat properly, you don't need a dietician, and if you train properly, you don't need a sports scientist. You can go into the fine-tuning elements of course, and I don't think there is any disadvantage in seeing a dietician even if you eat properly. But sports psychology is generally frowned upon. Even today, people say if a sportsperson needs a psychologist, there must be something wrong with them. But, from the time I first started working with Keith at Villa, it was serendipitous, because the week he spoke to me, I went out and played for England against Holland, came on at half time and 57 seconds later I was stretchered off with a posterior cruciate injury. I said to Keith that there was no point in doing anything with him because I was injured, but Keith said that this was the best time. So we spent three or four months working together, doing all the imagery work, and this really gave me time to get into it. Despite the fact that West Ham went down a couple of years later, my career was generally going in an upwards direction when usually what happens when you leave a club like Liverpool is that your form goes down. Mine, however, went up. I felt a lot stronger in myself. I had setbacks of course – everyone does. But I always say, don't worry about it, crack on.

What one-line sentence would you give to anybody aspiring to be the best they could be?

If you want to be the best, you have to know what it is you can be the best at. Anyone can play football, anyone can be their best at football, but they could be wasting so much time and effort when they might be a better basketball-player, for example, or they might get more enjoyment out of doing something else they are better at.

Which sportsman or sportswoman from another sport do you admire the most and why?

Brett Favre plays for the Minnesota Vikings in the NFL. He's 40 and I don't think he has missed a game since 2004. He's been hit hard, hammered, but he is still doing it. Randy Couture is a martial-arts professional, retired now, but at 45 years' old he was competing against 28- or 29-year-olds and holding his own. And both of these men are decent blokes. Simply because of their age, similar to me, they are good inspiration for me. From the world of football, in my very small world, I have a few friends who I get on with. Michael Owen is one of them and he has had a lot of setbacks, but even more than Michael, I would have to say David Beckham. Our careers have run a similar timeline and he is still playing at the highest level – and still hungry. We have always got on and since our re-introduction into the England squad, there is a bit more empathy there. The way he prepares and practises is a great example to young kids. He is the person I admire the most in the game.

KARL MORRIS SUMMARY

If you had the task of marketing the features and benefits of working with a sports psychologist, you could throw all of your brochures and flyers out of the window and just get people to read the words of David James. In the above chapter you can sense the sea-change in the fortunes of his football career from when David started to work on the mental game with the help of Keith Power. It seems surreal to me now why anyone who wants to be the best that they can in sport or business WOULDN'T look to train their mind in the way we all too readily accept the need to train the body and our technique.

It is fascinating how the work started with David at what would seem the most unlikely of times, whilst he was injured with cruciate ligament damage. Yet the power of harnessing mind and body together can be VERY powerful. There is much research to back up the reduction in injury recovery-time when using imagery combined with standard rehabilitation techniques.

When David talks about how he USED to respond to letting goals in, it is clearly from a man who now understands the benefit of the psychological training. If you feel great after a clean sheet but then terrible after letting a couple of goals in, then you are setting yourself up to ride a horrible, emotional rollercoaster that can be very damaging in the long run.

We all need to see that sport or business is something we DO, not something we ARE. We are more than our sporting performance. A good performance DOESN'T make us a better person and a bad performance doesn't make us a WORSE person. David James now seems to be better at finding this balance. This mindset actually allows us to become CHILDLIKE again, in the sense that we play the game or do the work for the game itself.

This is very different from people who become CHILDISH. Childish is when the toys go out of the pram after a poor performance or a bad shot, deal or outcome. We all need the skills to become more childlike and less childish. It is great testimony to David how he has had the courage and intelligence to explore some of his own demons and to be able to come out the other side a happier person and a BETTER goalkeeper. His story should be an education to us all.

ANTHONY (AP) McCOY, MBE

Anthony Peter McCoy MBE was born on 4th May 1974 in Moneyglass, County Antrim, Northern Ireland. He is commonly known as "AP" or "Tony" and is a horse-racing jockey. An impressive number of career wins has seen him widely regarded as the finest jump-jockey of all time.

McCoy was educated at St Olcan's High School in Randalstown, County Antrim. He left there at 15 and by the age of 17 his love of horses had led to his first winner on Legal Steps at Thurles on 26th March 1992. Since then he has amassed over 3,000 winners, becoming

Champion Jockey for the first time in 1996; a feat he has repeated in each of the last 14 years.

He has won the Cheltenham Gold Cup, Champion Hurdle, Queen Mother Champion Chase and King George VI Chase. Although he continues in his quest to win the Grand National, for punters up and down the country, he is seen as the safest pair of hands in the business.

QUESTIONS

What's your very first memory of horse-racing?

I can remember Shergar winning the Derby in 1981 – which would make me about seven. And I also remember Dawn Run winning the Gold Cup in 1984.

Who introduced you to horses and when did you first ride a horse?

My Dad had an interest in horses, although he never rode himself. He was a keen breeder of horses and even bred a horse called Thumbs Up which won at the Cheltenham Festival. A friend of my father was a trainer called Billy Rock who was a big influence. So I was introduced to horses from a very young age. In fact, I have a photo of me sitting on a horse when I was two years old. And it's odd, I have four sisters and one brother and there are no pictures of them on any horses. For some reason, I'm the only one that's ever been pictured sitting on a horse.

What other sports were you good at as a child and why did you decide to pursue horse-racing?

I was always very sporty. It was the only interest I had when I was young. I had no interest in school lessons or anything else to be honest. Sport was the thing: I loved football, I quite liked snooker and, obviously, I liked horses. Nowadays, I am keen on all sports – I can even follow cricket which I didn't think I'd ever be able to do!

How old were you when you first thought that you may be able to race for a living and turn your hobby into a full-time profession?

I knew, from about the age of 12, that racing was what I really wanted to do, but it wasn't until I was 14 or 15 that I began to think seriously that it was something I actually could do. I'm not an arrogant person, but I have always believed I could become a good jockey.

Who was the biggest single influence in helping you get there?

As time goes on, you realise that many people have had an influence on you and you learn from all of them. Of course, my Dad had the biggest influence on me from the very start and there was also Billy Rock, especially between the ages of 10 and 15. I was very lucky in that wherever I went, in racing terms, I was taught at all of the right places. At 15 I joined Jim Bolger's yard which, in my opinion, is the best schooler that any young person in horse-racing could have. I spent time there with great staff – the likes of Aidan O'Brien, Willie Supple, Ted Durcan, Paul Carberry, Seamus Heffernan, David Watchman – lots of people who had been successful in horse-racing. That was a very good schooling. When I came to England, I ended up with Toby Balding who was widely respected in the sport. He'd won Gold Cups, Grand Nationals, Champion Hurdles, the lot! From there I went to work for Martin Pipe, the most successful National Hunt Trainer ever, and from there I went to work for Jonjo O'Neill who was twice Champion Jockey, and a man who has had many battles in his life – including cancer. I have been very lucky to have worked for all these people, and in the best places in which to learn.

What was your big breakthrough moment in your career?

I'm not sure there was one big moment. Looking back, I think it was the fact that I moved from one stable to another that made the real difference. Each move brought me into contact with great trainers, great horses and great opportunities.

What sacrifices have you had to make in order to achieve success?

I left home when I was 15. Looking back, it's sad that I never got to grow up with my younger brothers and sisters - or any of my family for that matter. I left home 20 years ago, so I've been gone from home for longer than I lived there.

If there was one piece of advice that helped you become successful, what was it?

Martin Pipe always said to me that, even though I had ridden many winners before joining him, you can never stop learning; there will always be someone ahead of you. That was something which stuck in my mind – that there will always be someone who will achieve more than you; and of course there will always be someone coming along trying to do it better.

Do you have a set routine for mentally preparing for each race?

Not really; I take it as it comes. I am not in any way superstitious, although I am a bit of a dreamer. If there is one thing, it is that I always believe that I can win.

You've broken record after record. When you break a record, do you then look to see what the next milestone is?

I never look back. I don't ever think, well I've ridden 3,000 winners and that's great, well done, pat yourself on the back. I don't think like that. I want to ride 4,000 winners! That said, I'd probably have to ride until I'm 40 to achieve that and I don't think I'll be riding that long. But never say never; you always have to look ahead.

Can you describe the relationship between jockey and horse?

That's a very difficult question to answer. A lot of the horses that you ride, you have never seen before and will probably never see again. But for horses you ride a few times, I think the relationship has to come naturally. You have to get the 'feel' of the horse and the course – but remember that it's always the same objective, getting from start to finish quicker than anyone else.

When you know there is a lot of money being wagered on a horse you are riding, how does that make you feel?

If it's the people you are riding for, and if it's their money, you obviously want to win it for them. But to be perfectly honest, when I get on a horse, I want it to win for me. Whether there's one pound or one million pounds on the horse, it doesn't change my objective or outlook on how I go about the race. If someone close to me trusts me to win, that's their opinion. If they trust me to do that, then fair play to them. I would trust me to do it. Jockeys are not allowed to gamble, but I don't actually have any interest in it anyway. But if I did, I would want **me** to ride it. If someone said to me that they want to put a million pounds on a horse tomorrow, then I would want to have me riding for them. I don't mean that in a big-headed way but I'd rather take the so-called pressure of it or risk than give it to another jockey.

Do you think you can control your mind?

Yes, totally. I believe that sport - and life in general - is all about controlling the mind. It's about thinking positively all the time; negative things can get you down. It's hard because sometimes negative things happen, and it's difficult to not let them stick in your mind, but if they keep sticking in your mind, they'll be there and they will have an effect on your performance. Everyone makes mistakes in life – I know I have. But when you make mistakes, when you think that may affect how you are going to continue, the quicker you get that out of your head, the better.

How do you deal with doubt?

It might sound a simple thing to say but you should never have any doubt. Of course, even the strongest-minded person will have something creep in somewhere at some time. But you have to believe in yourself. You must never believe that, for whatever reason, someone else is going to do something better than you are.

What do you do when you feel nervous?

What are nerves? I think people that have performed well at big events don't get nervous. They get excited. They get butterflies, but I don't think that's a nervous thing; I think it's a big-occasion thing. People who suffer with nerves never really perform on the big stage. It's impossible not to get a nervous feeling in your body, but once an event starts, that all goes. For me, the worst thing that is going to happen is that I'm not going to win. It's more of a buzz thing, a big-occasion thing.

When you are under extreme pressure, how do you deal with that?

You have to believe in yourself and you have to eliminate the chances of making mistakes. You have to put yourself in the position where there's the smallest chance of something going wrong. If you do that with yourself, and the horse is properly prepared, then there's no reason why you won't win.

What is the best example of your being at your very best?

It's hard to know really, but winning the Queen Mother Champion Chase in 2000 on Edredon Bleu was pretty good. And the 2006 Champion Hurdle on Brave Inca. I'd thought for over a year that he would win the Champion Hurdle. In those situations there's obviously pressure on, but the pressure to prove your instincts right is as powerful as anything.

What do you dislike about your sport?

There is nothing I dislike about my sport. The only thing I dislike is myself being too heavy. If I could change anything about myself, I'd be a bit smaller and a bit lighter, but other than that, nothing.

What makes a bad day?

Last Sunday I had a horse which was going to win, but fell and had to be put down at the last. That's a bad day in terms of riding. But I have seen friends get killed at this sport - those are really bad days - so you have to be philosophical and put things into perspective.

Does winning a race get any less enjoyable with time?

Winning never gets less enjoyable. If anything, it gets even better. You'd think that I'd appreciate it less, but, believe it or not, I actually appreciate it even more. Maybe it's because I am getting older and, as with every sportsperson, there's a time-limit on everything.

What's been the most important ingredient in your achieving success?

Even though I think that when I ride a horse, I can ride it better than anyone else, I never take it for granted. I always feel that there might be more talented people out there. But as Muhammad Ali once said, you have to have the will and the skill, but the will must be stronger than the skill. To continue to try to be successful, you need to have a lot more will than skill. Skill will show on a big day, and maybe a few big days, but it won't keep you there for years. A lot of different sports-people will go through a lot of pain just to keep competing. To keep being successful at the top, you will go through a lot of pain, especially as a jump-jockey. But your pain-barrier is probably as important as any other aspect. People who have been at the top in sport for a long time will have times when their pain-barrier is tested to the limit. Those who carry on through the pain will stay at the top; the ones who don't, won't.

What would you do differently if you had your time again?

I've had a wonderful career so far and I wouldn't change anything or do things a lot different. But I wouldn't mind if someone could rewind the clock and I could have another go at it all!

For how long would you like to carry on riding?

Forever. But that's not really an option I suppose. Time is every sportsperson's enemy. I've always had the fear of being 35, even when I was 21. If anything, age probably makes you want to prove yourself even more. It probably makes you want to do even better.

What one-line sentence would you give to anybody aspiring to be the best they could possibly be?

You have to have belief. If you don't have belief, you have nothing. If you don't believe in yourself, how is anyone else going to believe in you?

Which sportsman or sportswoman from another sport do you admire the most and why?

Of course I admire Tiger Woods because of what he has achieved – how he has totally dominated his sport. I also admire people who have achieved great things without actually being the best - someone like Roy Keane who wasn't the best footballer ever, but achieved great things. Above all though, I'd probably say Ryan Giggs, even though I'm an Arsenal fan.

KARL MORRIS SUMMARY

It is always fascinating for me to look at the words and thoughts of the 'best of the best' in any sport and without a shadow of a doubt AP McCoy is the best of the best in the ultra-competitive world of horse-racing.

A number of key ingredients leap off the page here. It is clear that AP considers it absolutely vital to KEEP learning. His comment that he feels there might always be more talented people out there has driven him to fiercely seek out whatever knowledge he needs to keep ahead of his competitors. He clearly appreciates the value of mentors and good coaches along the way in his development to greatness. So many people in all walks of life make the grave error of thinking that they 'know enough' and then the process of stagnation begins to set in. He never takes his talent for granted. For me, this insatiable desire to keep improving is the bedrock of what AP considers to be vital to his success: his belief in his ability.

Too many people these days have a belief which is unfounded. AP believes in himself because his immersion in and dedication to his sport are TOTAL. It is fascinating he imagines that if HE had any wager on a race then he would want HIMSELF to be the jockey! That is REAL belief.

His take on nervousness is perfect, as he says, "What are nerves?" which clearly shows that, in his own mind, the feelings he gets in his body have been labelled as a good thing as opposed to something which should be dreaded. We all need to understand that these feelings are OK. It means we are alive, it means we are ready, it is not something to dread. IF you are prepared, as AP clearly is. He says "you have to eliminate the chance of making mistakes" and this is clearly a comment from someone who stacks the deck heavily in his own favour by preparing thoroughly and completely. Do not try and be confident based on words. It has to be backed up by action.

Wishing he could carry on riding forever, here is a man still in love with his sport. It is his reason to be. Despite all of the thousands of winners, he clearly still loves the feeling that winning gives him. "Never be complacent" is a very powerful message. We all need to celebrate our victories and be able to move on from defeat, to beat the pain. AP has this perfectly in balance: a love of winning and an ability to tough out failure.

SCOTT QUINNELL

Scott Quinnell was born on 20 August 1972 in Morriston, Wales. He was educated at Five Roads Junior School and Graig Comprehensive School in Llanelli. He is a former Welsh international rugby league and rugby union player, who played for Wigan (rugby league), Llanelli RFC, Llanelli Scarlets and Richmond, Wales and the British and Irish Lions (rugby union). He scored 11 tries for Wales and captained his country on seven occasions in rugby union. He was born dyslexic, and this was not diagnosed until he was 21 and it would be another 13 years before he found a treatment for it, after fellow rugby player Kenny Logan suggested that he enrol on the Dore Programme. This programme turned Quinnell's life around; he is now able to read and write, and works for the Dore Programme, alongside his media activities.

QUESTIONS

What's your first rugby memory?

My first memory is of putting my rugby boots on. I used to go down to Stradey Park (Llanelli's former ground) with my father. I would put on boots with metal studs and just run up and down the corridor in the clubhouse, the noise reverberating along the corridor. I just thought it was incredible. I can still remember the smell of liniment used by the players. I used to go down there to watch my Dad play on the odd occasion. You'd hear the team go out and hear the studs going down the tunnel, out onto the pitch. It brings back fantastic memories. Stradey has gone now, but every time I think about it I just think of those smells and that noise.

Who introduced you to the game?

My father did. He (Derek Quinnell) went on three British Lions tours, and played for Wales and the Barbarians. My uncle is Barry John, my godfather is Mervyn Davies, and my other brother's godfather is, J.J. Williams, all of whom played for Wales and the Lions. Another of my brother's godfather is Gareth Jenkins who coached Llanelli, Wales and the Lions. So, I was never going to get out of rugby; it was something that was in the blood.

Can you remember the first game you watched at a stadium?

It isn't a single game I can remember, but a whole lot of games at Stradey which sort of merge into one. When I was young, I used to stay a lot with my grandparents. When we moved down to Llanelli, when I was 14, the house was only 500 yards away from the club. I used to walk down, feeling big as I was able to have a Shandy Bass behind the bar, put a pound in the fruit machine, have a pasty, then go out to watch the game. I fell in love with the romantic side of the game, supporting, watching the players go from battle to battle. I don't remember a particular game, but I remember the people I went with and the time I had there.

Your father Derek had great success at Llanelli and was a three-time Lion. Was there any pressure to follow in his footsteps?

Never. I remember my father sitting me down and telling me that if I wanted to play rugby, he'd support me 100%. If I didn't want to play rugby, then he'd totally understand. I said, "Dad, just give me the boots." When I was very young, I used to tape my head, knees and ankles up just as my father used to, and I'd cut a cucumber up and use it as a gum shield. Because I struggled in school, rugby was my outlet. My mother and my grandfather often used to take me down to the games to watch my Dad, but there was never any pressure from my parents. Actually, the pressure came from outside influences, from the opposition and from people who didn't know me.

At school, you struggled enormously with everything, as your dyslexia hadn't been diagnosed. Just how difficult was it for you not being able to read or write?

You go to school to learn and, for me, junior school was a fantastic place. I had great teachers at that young age, especially Mrs Davies and Mr Rees. When I was struggling, they'd help me. My mate Martin Taffeutsareur who sat next to me, would help me. But if I was really struggling, I'd just go and play rugby. Then I went to secondary school, which is probably the hardest time of your life, where you have to move from class to class. A lot of people take it for granted that you go from English to Maths to Science to PE, but if you can't remember where the classrooms are, it becomes difficult. Not only are you assumed to be thick and stupid, you become lazy as well - you turn up five minutes late, that kind of thing. So, they were not great times for me. But I was lucky because I had rugby, which was my biggest coping strategy.

Everyone around you - teachers, your parents and friends - believed that the reason that you had no focus at school was because you were only focused on your rugby. This led to your parents banning you from playing for a while when you were 15. This really must have broken your heart, as rugby was your only escape from a world that you were afraid of?

I was lucky really. I played for my school when I was 15, but Mum and Dad said that I couldn't play for Llanelli as well because it was distracting me from my school work. It was a difficult year, as I'd have to go to watch matches, but not be able to take part. But when I got to 16, and things at school hadn't improved, they realised that at least I appeared happy in life, so they let me go back to playing rugby. They had banned me for the right reasons, so that I could get an education. Unfortunately, not knowing back then that I had dyslexia, there was nothing more they could do.

Given that you had such difficulties with everything related to school - concentration, reading, writing - would it be fair to say that your rugby benefited, as this was the channel which enabled you to release your frustration and aggression?

Yes, it probably did. I'd put so much time and effort into training and playing. Instead of doing homework, I went down to the gym and did weights. At the age of 18, I was probably as strong as guys who had been doing weights for ten years. I was physically very strong, and mentally quite strong too, in that I knew that was exactly where I should be. It's easy if you have a career-path you want to follow, even if it is challenging to try to improve yourself. It would have been quite easy to say if rugby was getting harder, I would go down another route, but I didn't feel that way, so rugby was the trade I plied.

At what point did you think that you would be able to earn a living as a professional rugby player?

It was when Mike Burton phoned my father and asked whether I would like to go to Wigan and play rugby league. So I went up there and met Jack Robinson, the Chairman. From that day on, my life changed. By then, I was doing very well in rugby union - I'd played for Wales nine times, played for Llanelli in cup finals - but what rugby league offered me was an opportunity to get paid to play rugby, not just playing as an amateur, basically for rugby's sake. Also, I had a young daughter Samantha, who was still a baby at the time, and I wasn't seeing a lot of her. I was working from 9 till 5, and training three nights a week, playing on a weekend, then going away for weeks on end with Wales. It was very difficult. Some weeks, I wouldn't see my daughter at all, because by the time I came home from work and training, she was already in bed. When I left in the morning, she wasn't up. So, changing rugby codes was a lifestyle move as much as it was for money.

Who was the biggest single influence in helping you in your career?

There's just so many. I've never been frightened of asking for help and I turned to so many people. For example, there was Wyn Oliver and Mr Owen at school to Alun Lewis, the youth coaches at Llanelli and Wales and my under 11's coach Mr John. There are so many to mention, but you take a little bit from all of them. If you are not frightened to ask for help, then you should not be frightened of getting the answers that sometimes you don't like, because that's one way of improving. I've been very lucky in the respect that my Dad was always there for me. I remember once, when I was young, I hadn't been picked for Llanelli, so I phoned Dad and, because he'd been through it all before, he knew exactly what to say. There are so many people out there that I owe a great debt to for helping me to where I am today.

What was your big breakthrough moment?

I was first capped by Wales in 1993 against Canada and I played against Scotland in 1994. But what everyone remembers was the day I scored a try against France that same year. After the game, David Gravell from Renault phoned me up and said, "Scott, would you like a sponsored car?" Soon afterwards, I got calls from both Wigan and Leeds to see if I would like to play rugby league. So that was the moment I realised I had been elevated from a club player to an international.

Was that the seminal moment for you, then?

Yes, I think it probably was, but it all started on the first day I got into the gym. There were days when I went to the gym and I'd have to drive home in first gear as I couldn't change gear because my chest and my shoulders were burning. There was David Fox, a great hooker at Llanelli who, when I didn't feel like doing the 250-metre run at training, he'd call me all the names under the sun, grab hold of me and make sure I did it. People like David are, for me, the unsung heroes. Every time I fell down, David would pick me up and drag me along. Although it culminates in a particular game, people don't always see that the underlying factor is that it was generated maybe ten years prior to that.

What do you remember of that day, then?

In sport, sometimes you have to be lucky; the ball has to come to you, the bounce must go for you. I'd done things in that game that I'd probably done 100 times for Llanelli before. Gary Player once said that the harder you work, the luckier you get, and people in sport say you need a slice of luck. In rugby, the harder you work, the more times you are likely to see the ball in a game, which means the more influence you can have – and I can tell you I worked hard that day! After the game, I went out with the other boys in the team, and my wife Nicola, for a couple of beers. Then, on the Sunday, I went home and saw my daughter Samantha. It was fantastic. It was a great game, but we still had to play Ireland and England. As a sportsman, if you dwell too long on things that go well, something will come along and come crashing down and put everything back into perspective.

What sacrifices have you had to make in order to achieve success?

It's the simple things like not going out drinking with your mates on a Saturday night. Looking back though, I don't feel as if I made any sacrifices as such, because it was a way of life. The people who made sacrifices are my family - my three children, and my wife in particular. When everyone else is going to Bonfire Night or the school play, when everyone else is there for the kids' birthdays, I'm not always there. I've missed hundreds of different things over the years which mean so much to me and the family. At times, my wife has felt like she was a single parent. They have sacrificed for me and I have never taken that for granted and I hope they know that.

If there was one piece of advice that helped you become successful, what was it?

I was constantly told not to give up. The position on the field which I played meant that I was always being knocked over, which eventually takes its toll. But if you give up and don't keep on hammering away at it, then there's no point in being there in the first place. I've been quite single-minded in that way. There have been times when I couldn't run, but I was very fortunate that I had excellent coaches, fitness-coaches, physiotherapists, family and other players around me who understood that, even if I had been told to give up playing rugby, I simply couldn't have, because it was the only thing I could do. I had arthritis in one of my knees and was told I probably wouldn't run again, so I was very fortunate to get another seven years out of it.

Did you have a set routine for mentally preparing before each game?

Well, preparation always started with beans and toast for lunch! In the dressing room, two minutes before kick-off, I would have Deep Heat rubbed all over my body. If I wasn't captain, I'd always run out last but one. Sportsmen tend to be very superstitious. If things go right for you, you keep on doing it - if they don't, you change it.

Do you think you can control your mind?

Yes, you can certainly control your mind. You can go through barriers that sometimes you put in front of yourself – and the hardest one is controlling your mind. A lot of people fail in sport because they put their own barriers up around themselves. What you have to do is deconstruct those barriers and set yourself realistic goals. If you are trying to knock down a big building, you don't take a big run at it; you take small pieces out of it. And if you go for the foundations first, it's not going to happen. I've always been a big believer in goal-setting. I write down my biggest goal on top of a piece of paper and then write maybe 15 or 20 smaller goals beneath that to indicate how you may achieve the big one. You then have to keep chipping away until you eventually reach that big goal.

What do you feel is your most destructive emotion and how do you deal with it?

I am an emotional person, which I actually see as a strength. I live and die by the sword. I'm a very fiery character, which especially came to the fore on the rugby field. I didn't take any nonsense - if you hit someone, you expect someone to hit you back. If they hit you first, you have to hit them back. It could be said that my weakness is that I am over-emotional, but it's probably one of my biggest strengths as well.

When you were told that you would be captaining Wales for the first time, you had very mixed feelings. Above all, you were terrified of having to make a speech after the game. You couldn't sleep at night because you were so worried about it. How did you manage to get through during this period?

I got through it just by the overriding emotion of being the captain of Wales. There have only been a few players who have been asked to captain their country. To have that accolade was incredible. It's something you don't even dream of when you grow up. When Graham Henry, the Welsh coach at the time, asked me for the first time, my immediate reaction was, "yes, of course", but then I quickly realised that I would have to stand up after the game in front of 150 people and make a speech. The first two days after accepting the captaincy I got no sleep. Then I said to myself that I should just get through the game, then worry about the speech afterwards. It was no problem to walk out in front of 85,000 people and play rugby, but standing up in front of 150 is another matter altogether. But my great pride and passion for the captaincy allowed me to take small steps to overcoming my fear of talking.

As a player, what did you do when you felt nervous?

There are different types of nerves. There are positive nerves before the game, the ones that if you do not have before the game, there is something wrong. If you haven't got those butterflies which turn into dragons before you walk out into the Millennium Stadium, then there's no point playing the game. Then there are the nerves which come from self-doubt. Am I good enough to be on the park? Players are always looking for reassurance. I've been very lucky in that I have been confident in my own limited ability and understand my own ability whenever I am asked to perform.

What is the best example of you being at your very best?

Most of the best games I played were for the Llanelli Scarlets in the European Cup. I always loved playing in France. And I loved playing at home in front of a 15,000 crowd. If I had to pick one game though, it would either be that 1994 Test against France or the First Lions Test in 2001, when I scored a really important try. In both those games I stood up and rose to the occasion.

When you had to pull out of the 1997 Lions tour through injury before the first test match, you set yourself the personal goal that you had to make the next tour in 2001. In the First Test at Brisbane, after you had scored a try, you gave a "nod" celebration. What did the nod mean?

It was a thank you to everyone who had contributed to my personal goal. Although goals are personal, you have to break those goals down and you have to overcome the barriers. In 1997, I was playing for Richmond but wasn't enjoying playing there, so I decided that I needed to move. The Llanelli Scarlets offered me terms, and I felt that was a good move. I played better rugby there and, although I took a 45% pay cut to go back, I was happier there. I wanted to play for the side that I had always supported. My family was happy. It was then that I was diagnosed as having arthritis in my knee and I had to have an operation, and was told that I would have to stop playing by the doctor. But I refused. I just couldn't do it; it was the only thing I knew. Because I couldn't run every day, I'd do two or three sessions in the pool. The physios were great; I had a session every day. Peter Herbert, the fitness coach, and then later, Wayne Proctor, were both fantastic. They would meet me after working with the other players at half past six in the pool and I'd train. Then I'd go back to the club and do my weights and watch the boys train just to feel a part of it. Graham Henry came to see me at that time and thought I shouldn't do so much with Wales – all of which contributed to me finally getting selected on the 2001 Lions tour. Then when we were on the tour in Australia, with my family and my friends all around me and supportive – well, I worked out a couple of years later, that nod was for everyone who had helped me achieve that goal. Although it was my personal goal to play in that

Test match, to score a try and win the first Test match, it was an incredibly powerful emotion and that nod was to over 250 people who had helped me along the way.

What's been the most important ingredient in your achieving success?

It's been the people around me; that, and not being frightened of asking for help and not being frightened to take criticism. I have also not been frightened of putting myself on the line, both mentally and physically. I had a great desire to be the best I could be. Sport is hugely physical, but the mental side of the game is massive: to push yourself through barriers at times when things are going badly, to think of my family and the people who loved me, thinking that I couldn't let them down was always a challenge.

Aged 34, after a recommendation from Kenny Logan, you enrolled yourself and your children, Lucy and Steele, on the Dore Programme. What exactly is this?

The Dore Programme helps people that have cerebellum issues. The cerebrum is the part of your brain that deals with work, and the cerebellum is like a fuse-box in the brain, acting as the librarian and storing all the information you need to re-use in everyday life, such as driving, remembering your way from A to B, eating, co-ordination, reading and writing; basically, anything you do. It's an exercise-based programme that stimulates the sensory system, the visual system and the vestibular system. That then helps in hand-eye co-ordination, spatial awareness, gross motor-control, fine motor-control. It helps people with labels such as dyslexia, dyspraxia, and ADHD.

Having successfully gone through the Programme, you were then in a position for the first time in your life, to read and write properly. Was this a Eureka moment for you?

I cried when the doctor mentioned to me, for the first time, that I was within the normal range for reading and writing. I cried because, at the age of 34, no one had ever told me that before. I'd been told I was quite a good ball-carrier, that I could play a bit of rugby and I was quite a good sportsman, but no one had ever complimented me on my reading and writing. Before I started the Programme I had a reading age of 7.

To then be told a year later that I was within the normal range for reading and writing was a very powerful emotion.

You are now actively involved in the Programme; just how rewarding is it being able to help other people completely turn their lives around?

It's strange. When I was younger, I thought playing rugby was as good as it can get. Retiring at the age of 32, not being able to read or write, struggling still to provide for my family, I started to work for Sky Television and they have been fantastic. They really helped me with my reading and writing difficulties as well. I have been fortunate to have had the opportunity to work on programmes like The School of Hard Knocks, to go to colleges, comprehensive and junior schools, and talk to people in education and in the workplace - and people out of the workplace - about dyslexia, dyspraxia, ADHD and so on. It is massively rewarding. When I was 13, I used to go home and cry in my bedroom. I couldn't understand why I was different from everybody else. I don't want people thinking in this day and age that they are on their own. I want them to be able to ask for help and get help. There are a lot of people doing an awful lot of good work but we are still nowhere near where we need to be.

What advice would you give to anyone who thinks they, or maybe a child of theirs, may have dyslexia, dyspraxia or some other disability?

The biggest thing for me is awareness. People need to understand why someone is struggling. If they go to the Dore Programme's website, (www.dore.co.uk), there is a lot of information on learning difficulties. We need to break down the barriers and understand why someone struggles in a certain way, so they can then ask for help. I always go back to the importance of being able to stick your hand up and ask. Parents, teachers, coaches, friends should all be able to help you. You should never feel that you are on your own.

What one-line sentence would you give to anybody aspiring to be the best they could be?

Never give in.

Which sportsman or sportswoman from another sport do you admire the most and why?

Arnold Schwarzenegger. He has always been so determined. Look at him as a sixteen-year-old coming over from Austria to America. He was determined to be the best, so he pushed himself and set himself goals. He won five Mr Universe and seven Mr Olympia titles. He said he would run for office, even before he was able to run for office, not only in sport, but elsewhere, being the Governor of California he has wanted to help people. At the moment, people who weren't born in America can't become President, but who'd say he won't be in the future?

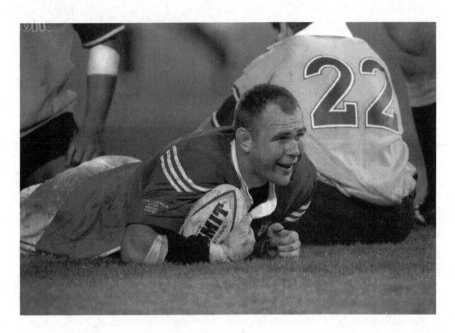

KARL MORRIS SUMMARY

I once heard a story which suggested Tiger Woods has stored in his mind a hundred of his best shots so that, when he is faced with a certain situation on the course, one of the shots would spring into his mind. The feeling being that it is as if he has already played the shot. It doesn't surprise me, as I am convinced that our memory, and how we use it, is one of the single biggest factors in how good we become at a particular sport. Woods has said he feels that 'the secret' is instantly to recall past success and to let go of failure.

It is very clear that the moment Scott Quinnell thinks about the sounds of the legendary Stradey Park, the distinctive click of the metal rugby-studs, the smell of liniment, he is taken back to a very happy place in his mind. The beginning of his sporting life is so clearly etched deep into his memory as a wonderful time. It is a memory which clearly inspired him to want to keep playing rugby despite some real setbacks with injury.

It is so important we take great care with our memories. When high emotion is involved, we store those memories in a different part of our neural networks. The golden rule for me should be that we need to increase our emotion on things we do well and to decrease as much as possible the emotion on things which don't turn out as we wish. This is a skill that can be developed.

How clear it is that Scott has a complete understanding of the need that we all have to ask for help from others. To be able to sit down and discuss issues with people who have been there before is not a sign of weakness, it is an essential commodity to becoming the best you can be. It is absolutely no exaggeration to say lives can be turned around completely by the right word, the right sentence, at the right time.

I can only begin to imagine what incredibly powerful inspiration Scott must now provide to those people who may have been labelled in the past as a result of learning or reading difficulties. It seems he has found a purpose which stretches far beyond the scope of sport, but it is a message that is carried with such authority because of his achievements within sport.

DENNIS TAYLOR

Dennis Taylor was born on 19th January 1949 in Coalisland, County Tyrone, Northern Ireland. He was educated at the Primate Dixon Memorial Boys' School. He is a retired snooker-player, and current BBC snooker-commentator.

Taylor is well known for his sense of humour and his trademark over-sized glasses. He won the hearts of a gripped nation by winning the

1985 World Snooker Championship, beating the seemingly invincible Steve Davis on the black ball in the final frame in what is one of sport's greatest moments. He was 6-times Irish Champion, Benson & Hedges Champion, Rothmans Grand Prix Champion and was Champion of World Champions in 1986.

QUESTIONS

What's your first memory of snooker?

It was at a club called Jim Joe's. It was a privately owned club with two tables and there was a little black-and-white television and Joe Davis was playing Fred Davis. This was in the late 1950s and early 1960s and I was fascinated watching it. I was 9 at the time. I remember looking into the club through the door and the coloured balls on the table fascinated me, too. I was a good little boy and used to sit and hold the rest for the grown-ups who were playing. Eventually, they let me stand on a lemonade box and have a shot. That's how it started.

Who were your boyhood heroes?

When I moved to England when I was 17, John Spencer had just won the World Amateur Championship. He was a big influence and I got invited to play John by a local newspaper.

Where did you start to learn the game properly?

At that time, I was doing all sorts of jobs. My first job was working twelve-hour shifts in a paper-mill, for seven days a week. I used to stay with my aunt and I would come home after the 12-hour shift, get on the bus after a bit of tea, and I'd go down to Blackburn and play for a couple of hours. That was my proper introduction to the game and I started to improve very quickly. I always picked a better player to practise with. There weren't any coaches in those days; you would learn to play through watching other people. After working the shifts, I then took an office job, and then I worked in a shop selling domestic appliances. After that I managed a snooker-club before turning full-time professional.

How often did you play at that time?

I was practising quite a lot. When I was 18 I was working in the shop, and Alex Higgins moved over to Blackburn. We used to go off and practise together and, on my half-day off, we'd play all day. I played thousands of frames against Alex in the early days.

At what point did you tell yourself that you wanted to play snooker for a living?

When I got to the age of 19 or 20, I'd got to quite a high standard and I had seen people like John Spencer turn professional, and I thought I could have a crack at it. When I turned professional in the early 1970s, there were only 16 professional players in the game. It was quite a big step, but I had the job at the snooker club as well, so I'd manage the club one week and then I would try and get some exhibition games for the week I was off, which wasn't easy in those days. The big turning point was when I was married with two children, I had 200 quid in the bank, and I paid my own way to go to Canada to play in the Canadian Open in 1974. I couldn't even afford to stay in a hotel, so I stayed with the organiser at his house, but that meant that I could put a lot of practice in. I got to the final of the Canadian Open and in an exhibition match, I made a unique 3-frame break of 349, without missing a shot. I cleared 105 in the first frame. In the next frame, I broke and fluked a ball and cleared the table with a 134 break. In the next frame, my opponent broke and I then made a 110 break. This generated a lot of publicity alongside getting to the final of the Canadian Open – and from this I got an invitation to go onto [BBC TV's] *Pot Black*. I got to the final of *Pot Black* in 1975 and that was me on the ladder, and people then knew my name.

How were finances at the time?

You had to fund everything yourself and they then moved the 1975 World Championship to Australia. So I had to raise the money to go and play there. I partly funded that by doing shows for the local brewery. I'd get 20 quid a night. That money went towards the air fare to Australia, where I got to the semi-final. That was another stepping-stone.

Was it a personal goal of yours to become World Champion one day? If so, when did you set yourself this goal?

When you turn professional, the main goal should be to become World Champion. That's what you are in the game for. Unfortunately, there are a lot of players who maybe just haven't got that driving ambition and are quite happy to make a living, as is the case in the golf world. You need to have that extra drive to want to go on and become World Champion. I was hindered with a pretty bad eyesight and I used to have to take my glasses off to play. The specialist could never understand how I did that. In 1979 I started to wear contact lenses and the difference that made was incredible. I got to the final that year and should have won it, but I lost to Terry Griffiths. I had beaten Steve Davis and Ray Reardon. But I could only keep the lenses in for 3 or 4 hours at a time and I knew then that I needed an aid which I couldn't get with the lenses, so that's how the glasses came about. I would never have won the World Championship without the big glasses. Jack Karnehm used to commentate for the BBC. He was a player too and his family business was making spectacle frames. The ones I won the world title with he made by hand. There were a few faults with them, but they worked for me. You could normally make a pair of specs in an hour, but I ended up spending two days with Jack making these ones. They gave me the confidence to go on and win the Championship.

After two semi-final losses in the World Championship in 1975 and 1977, you made it to the final in 1979, but were beaten 24-16 by Terry Griffiths. Did this defeat make you more determined to win the trophy one day?

It really did. I should have won it in 1979. I was 15-13 in front but I had a terrible last day and Terry played well. And I thought to myself, you've got to the final now, so next time there is no reason why you can't go on and win it. But I had to wait another six years to get back in the final again.

In 1984, you lost in the semi-final to Steve Davis and later that year, your mother died. When you lost her, did your mental outlook on your profession change in any way?

Absolutely. After my mother died, I wasn't even going to play in the next tournament. I just didn't want to know about snooker. My mother was only 62 and she died suddenly. But my family all persuaded me to go and play in the Rothmans Grand Prix. And immediately my attitude changed - I was no longer worried about losing. I had a different perspective on the game, and I just went out and played the best snooker of my career. My mother was there with me in spirit throughout the whole final, which helped to boost me psychologically. When things went wrong, I just sat there and had a little chat with her. That carried on and I had four years where I won tournaments all over the world. It took me a while to develop a killer instinct, which you have to have, and my mother's death started it all. Even when I beat Steve Davis, I was chatting to her between frames. A lot of people were beaten before they got their cue out of the case when playing against Steve. He used to dominate the table with the way he would walk around it. I would pretend to be looking at him, but I was focusing underneath the table as I didn't want to see what he was doing. From a psychological point of view, I wanted to have myself ready for when I went to the table. Sitting watching someone playing the table frame after frame is not good, so I tried not to focus on what he was doing.

You talk about killer instinct. How would you summarise this?

With the experience I had, I had a few run-ins with Alex Higgins and beat him to the Irish title. Playing against him gives you a killer instinct, because he'd just hammer you otherwise. Steve Davis as well – he would hammer you. So you have to try and develop a killer instinct. It comes with experience. Some people will get it quicker than others. It took me a little bit longer, but once I had it, I just didn't like losing.

Having won your first major ranking-event later that year, in the same season, you then reached the World final to be drawn against Steve Davis. At 8 frames to nil down, where were you mentally?

Throughout the whole of the championship, my good friend Trevor East was with me, but on the Saturday afternoon he was away and I lost all seven frames in the first session. The Crucible was a really lonely place at that time. I wasn't doing anything wrong though, which is why I kept believing. Trevor then came back and was with me for the rest of the match and he was a great support to me. Even when Steve won the first frame in the second session, I was psyched up and I told myself not to give up, as it was the first to 18 frames. Mentally I stayed strong even though I wasn't getting any chances. Then I did get a chance. Steve went for a risky green which wobbled in the jaws and I cleared up to win my first frame. Even though he won the next to make it 9-1, I suddenly got that fire in my belly and I kept him in his seat for the whole of the evening and I won the last 6 frames of the session. Once I got the chance, I took it. It would have been so easy to have given up. A lot of people at 8-0 down would have given in, but I thought I just wasn't going to do that. I battled and battled, stayed very positive, although Steve's supporters started to get to me a little bit. But, actually, this started to help me. I talked to the two people sat behind me throughout the final. I didn't know who they were, but I kept chatting to them and I kept telling them that he wasn't going to beat me.

Quite incredibly, you battled back to take the match into the final frame, tied at 17-17. Looking back on it now, has there ever been anything in your life which comes close to the pressure you were under during those final 68 minutes at the Crucible?

No, you couldn't have matched that. The way that last frame panned out was simply incredible. Steve was going whiter by the shot and I was going redder by the shot. The pressure was that intense. Towards the end of the frame, I remember the last four colours and it didn't matter where the balls were going to finish, I was going to have a go at them. I didn't want to play a safety shot and I was very positive. It was a good thing getting my brain to be positive. It would have been so easy to have been cagey, and play safety shots. I pulled them off. I potted a fantastic brown, a tricky blue and pink, and even tried to double the black, I was still that positive. All the crowd cheered the double as they thought the black was in. I should have played a safety shot. The only thing which would come close to matching that tension was my first night on *Strictly Come Dancing* - coming down the stairs to dance live in front of 10 million people. That was the nearest thing to the Crucible.

Ted Lowe famously commented when there was just the black left on the table that he had never known an atmosphere quite like it. Did you enjoy being in this pressure-cooker environment?

I did; it was just incredible. I think I was more nervous for the people watching though. I was 36, which was probably my last chance to win the World Championship, and I don't think an older person has won it since then. It was just so intense. That all came out when the black finally went in. I stamped the cue, held it above my head, then I started wagging my finger. The one that came close to that was playing Alex Higgins in the Masters Final. Once again that shows you how you can mentally win a match that you should have lost. I was 8-5 down and again, Trevor East was with me and Trevor told me that Alex's manager had just ordered champagne to celebrate Alex's first tournament win for two years. I came back in from the break and I won the last four frames. I was determined there was no way he was going to beat me. That's why a lot of sports people – especially multiple winners like Stephen Hendry and Steve Davis - have that all the time. To hold onto that for 10 years, as both of them did, was fantastic. They were so strong mentally. I had it for a period of four years, where I was mentally very strong.

After Steve Davis played an excellent safety-shot to take the black to the other end of the table, you went back to your table and took a while to dry your hands and take some time out. Were you just trying to relieve some of the pressure and calm yourself?

Yes I was. Normally I was renowned for having a crack with the crowd in certain situations, but towards the end of that frame, I was trying to relieve some of the tension. The next shot I think I tried to double the black from one end of the table to the other. I was going for all sorts of things.

Did you have the first chance to win on the black?

Yes, I had the first proper chance to pot the black down past the green spot. I was thinking, I have all these years' experience behind me, now just put it into this one shot, keep your head still, push the cue through four or five times, then through in a straight line and you're World Champion. I was thinking positively. The pressure was so intense that I jerked at it, and missed it. It came back out and Steve should have potted the one after that. It just shows you. Mentally, he was the strongest player snooker has ever had, but he told me afterwards that when he walked across the Crucible floor to play that black he felt that his legs had gone, like they were somebody else's. When he put his hands on the table, he said that it was like someone else's arms. He ended up over-compensating which just shows you what the mind can do. At that point, I thought it was all over for me. I pushed my glasses above my head and mentally I was down on the floor. I'd fought back and kept fighting back, and suddenly it was there for me, and then it wasn't. I watched Steve's cut into the bottom pocket. As soon as Steve had taken the shot, he stood up immediately and put his hand up to his head. He knew immediately that he had missed. Under pressure, you always miss that particular shot on the thick side, but Steve's brain was working overtime and he thought he mustn't hit it thick, so he hit it thin.

When you lined up to take your final shot to win the match, did you tell yourself that this is going in? Or did you think if it goes in I win, if it doesn't I don't? What was your mindset approaching this pot?

If you ever watch that shot, it looks like it is on freeze frame I took so long over it. I thought I am not going to miss this. Instead of gripping the cue tightly, I just let it rest on my four fingers which meant that I couldn't snatch at it. I took ages. When the ball went in, it's hard to describe exactly what it felt like. It was unbelievable. 13 years trying to become World Champion. And when I started stamping the cue, I thought "I'm World Champion". It was an unbelievable feeling. Nothing would come close to that again. Steve says that he remembers that more than the six he won. As the years go on, people still talk more and more about it. You get young people today coming up and talking about it – that they were four or five at the time, but how they were allowed to watch the game.

Do you think you can control your mind?

Yes I do. I did a bit of work with Paul McKenna who I'd say would be as good a sports psychologist as anybody. He's great to work with, as he gets you in the right frame of mind. Had I carried on playing the game longer, I would have worked even more on the mental side of the game – like keeping myself positive or sitting upright in the seat. Look at Peter Ebdon – bolt upright - whereas Ronnie O'Sullivan sometimes is not, slumped, which is sending out signals to his opponent. Players do glance over and look at you. Even though you are not at the table, how your posture is plays a big part. Towards the end of my career, when I took shots on, all you would picture in your mind is where the white was going after that pot. So the ball was automatically in the pocket before you played it. Occasionally, you might have missed one, but it's a bit like a putt in golf. The really strong putters will already see themselves bending down and picking the ball out of the hole. Many years ago I went to see a hypnotist, but I didn't really get on with that, so I read books like *The Inner Game of Golf* [by W. Timothy Gallwey]. In basketball, half the team visualised the ball going in the basket and the other half of the team were practising getting the ball in the basket. In the competition after, the ones who were visualising hit more baskets. Sprinters always run the race before it is run. You can't do that in snooker, but you can with individual shots. A lot of the players now work more on the mental side of the game, whereas in my day, there was very little of that in the game. Golf is now rife with sports psychologists.

What do you do when you feel nervous?

I used to take a few little breaths to keep my breathing under control. I wouldn't focus on what my opponent was going to do, but just what I was going to do if I got a chance. That always helped me to relax a bit.

What do you feel is your most destructive emotion and how do you deal with it?

Just like with a lot of the players, it would be frustration and anger; when you mess up a shot and have to go and sit down. Ronnie O'Sullivan missed a shot once and then scratched his forehead and left marks there! Jimmy White once bashed the ball with his cue which is how you feel inside and a lot of players feel like that. Controlling those emotions and having a good temperament is the big thing. Golf and snooker are similar in that respect, as you are hitting a stationary ball. Controlling your temperament plays a big part.

As a percentage, how much of playing snooker is in the mind and how much is skill and talent?

I would give the mind 80%. There were loads of great players – even as an amateur – I played against who were brilliant, but you put them in front of half a dozen people, and they couldn't do it. Psychology plays a huge part in it.

Of all the skills and strengths required to play snooker at the top level, which is the most important?

You have to have the ability to start with. But confidence is the biggest thing, as you can see with Ronnie. Being able to control your emotions, that all comes with confidence.

If your opponent is at the table for long periods of time and you are just sat watching, how difficult is it to stay in the right place mentally and be ready for your next visit to the table?

That's the toughest thing to do in the game. It's all about trying to control your mind. Some players are so intense and watch what their opponent is doing all the time. To me, that doesn't do you any good. You have to try to get yourself right for when you go to the table. One technique I had was to visualise one of my happy memories from back home. In my mind I'd find a field where I used to go and lie on a nice sunny day. I used to do that to get myself in a nice frame of mind. The other thing I used to do was to remember some of my best performances, especially against Steve Davis. I remember I came back from 4-0 down and made three century breaks in four frames, and I'd focus on things like that. Pick one of your best performances and think of that. It's like putting the right information into the computer.

What is the hardest part of being a professional snooker player?

Even though the travelling was very, very enjoyable – I travelled all over the world – it was quite tough. I might have to travel to Bangkok or Hong Kong, and then have to play the next day. I loved every minute of my snooker career, so there is nothing really bad about it.

How can snooker get back to the dizzy days of the 1980s?

It's difficult as people always compare it to when I played Steve in the final with 18 million people watching. You are never going to get that now. Snooker still gets its fair share of viewing figures. They are currently considering a game of six reds – a bit like cricket has done with Twenty20 - but I don't think they need to tinker with snooker. It's good as it is. You have young Chinese players coming through and it's still very popular on television. You could possibly jazz it up a little, but there's not a lot you can change.

What's been the most important ingredient in your achieving success?

Winning my first title helped, of course. But I have always had a sense of humour, always liked to have a bit of fun with people. If something happened, I would always react to it. That played a big part. For years, people asked me how I would like to be remembered and I would answer that I would like to be remembered for putting a bit of fun into the game. I enjoyed it, I had a crack with people, as well as being very competitive. I will always be remembered for potting that black in the Steve Davis final, and I'd rather be remembered for that than for having a sense of humour!

If there was one piece of advice that helped you become successful, what was it?

There was a Welsh snooker player called Mario Berni who passed away recently. Mario was a great philosopher and he gave me a great bit of advice. He said when you are at the table, you have to learn to be able to beat your own ego. I thought that was great. When you first go in and you are on television playing a match, you take some shots on and you know you shouldn't take them on – and you are doing it for the crowd and for the television. He said, if you can beat your own ego and refuse that urge to play a reckless shot, you will win more games. You won't hand the game away. That was a great bit of advice.

What one-line sentence would you give to anybody aspiring to be the best they could be?

It's all about focus. Whatever you want to do, you have to focus. Don't ever think that you can't achieve it, because as soon as you do that, you have no chance whatsoever. You have to tell yourself you can do it, that you are going to do it and then keep telling yourself you can do it. If you put the hard work in, you will get there. I only had £200 and I was determined to do well. Don't be afraid to take the chance as well. The legendary Joe Davis gave me that advice. He said play the percentages, don't over risk it, but don't go negative either. Find that balance, which someone like John Higgins has.

Which sportsman or sportswoman do you admire the most and why?

I admire Stephen Hendry as he is the greatest player that has ever picked up a cue, but Ronnie O'Sullivan is awesome. Ronnie is the only player I would use the word genius about. He is a genius on a snooker table. I have played him where he has switched hands and cleared the table with a 135 break, playing every shot with his opposite hand. I'd have loved the great Joe Davis to have seen Ronnie play. He is without doubt something special, but Stephen Hendry is the greatest.

From outside the world of snooker, not because he was my best man, Ian Woosnam, when he won the Masters in 1991. I thought that was awesome. The moment he knocked that putt in to win the Masters, that was an unbelievable moment for me. I was also ringside when Barry McGuigan beat Pedroza at Queen's Park Rangers football ground. I'd just won the World Championship and I needed a police escort into the fight, as the ground was full of Irish people and the crowd went berserk when I went in ringside. They were two great sporting moments for me – but Woosie's would be the special one.

KARL MORRIS SUMMARY

It could be said the truly iconic moments in sports are few and far between. Moments which live on in the collective memory long after the event has been played out. Bannister breaking the 4-minute mile, Doug Sanders missing a four-foot putt for the Open at St Andrews, Gareth Edwards scoring rugby's 'greatest' try for the Barbarians against the All Blacks.

We could all think of a couple, but there is no doubt that Dennis Taylor potting the final black to win the World Championship against Steve Davis would be in most people's list of sport's greatest moments. The black went in, Dennis stood bent-legged wielding his cue above his head and the defining moment of becoming World Champion was his.

These 'white-heat' moments are an inspiration to us all and can be the very moment that a passing interest in a sport can become a lifetime passion. Time and again, within the pages of this book, we hear great stars talking about the importance of working on your mind.

Many of the great players of the past had wonderful psychological tools and techniques, perhaps without realising it. Maybe it took them until the end of their career to work it out.

Dennis says that if he had the time again he would work more on the mental aspects. I think it is ridiculous when people say you either 'have it or you haven't. One of the great discoveries from neuroscience is the concept of 'brain plasticity', the ability of the brain to change. Up until as recently as 15 years ago most neuroscientists would have told us that past a certain age we pretty much had what we had. This has now been proved to be a myth. Your brain CAN change.

It isn't literally plastic, of course, but it can be altered by training in specific ways. A lot of the tools that you are learning from these great sportsmen and women will allow you to change your habitual responses and learn to react differently, to become the player that you are truly capable of being. Take particular notice when Dennis talks about the importance of posture. The brain and the body are in a constant two-way dialogue. Change your body and you change your mind. Be very aware of your body-language when you play your sport. You are sending out a very powerful message to others but perhaps most importantly you are sending out an even more powerful message to the key player in the drama: YOURSELF. Have the intention always of 'taking charge of your body language'.

A great technique - and one we should all be better at - is to constantly replay, in the theatre of our mind, the times when we have done well. Dennis drew on his century breaks against Steve Davis when his back had been well and truly pinned to the wall. When you do something well, log it in your memory bank. Better still, write it down. This isn't positive thinking but positive reflection. One has a limited effect; the other is immensely powerful. Use it wisely.

PHIL "THE POWER" TAYLOR

Philip Douglas Taylor was born on 13th August 1960. He was educated at Mill Hill Junior School in Tunstall, Stoke-on-Trent, and Stanfield Technical High School. He is a professional darts player.

Taylor played darts in the pubs in Stoke-on-Trent and was spotted by former World Champion Eric Bristow. Bristow duly sponsored Taylor on the condition that the money was repaid at a later date. This enabled

Taylor to practise full time and to enter low-level tournaments. By 1990, he had qualified to play in the World Championships for the first time. Incredibly, Taylor reached the final where he was matched against Bristow himself. Taylor, available at 125-1 pre-tournament, beat Bristow 6 sets to 1 and was crowned World Champion for the first time. This was the beginning of a remarkable career which has seen him win more than 52 major titles and a stunning 15 World Championships. In total he has won over 130 tournaments, over twice as many as any other player in the game.

QUESTIONS

What's your first memory of darts?

My first memory is my parents playing when I was a kid. They were keen players. When I was little, you didn't have a television unless you were really posh, which we weren't, so most people made up their own entertainment. You'd play cards or dominoes or throw hoops, and we played darts. The dartboard was in the front room at home. In our house, you couldn't go upstairs, because it was falling down and derelict. I think my parents paid £100 for the house. But my mother knew that if we lived there for a couple of years, you would get a council house after that in a nice area, which is what we did.

Is it right that your father tapped in to the electricity supply next door as he couldn't pay the bills?

My mother eventually had a television fitted by Rediffusion, and the man came and fitted it all in, he put the wire across as it was, because there was no aerial on Rediffusion, and when we plugged it in, there was no electricity. So we ran a cable into next door's supply. My mother used to run a catalogue and the lady next door would buy goods off my mother, maybe a few shillings a week, which my mother would pay for her, and in return, she gave us electricity for free.

Who got you into the game?

My father, who I used to play with once a week. He used to play for a club, the CIU Club. I played on a Tuesday in the CIU League, and I really enjoyed that, as I didn't go out very often. I was 25 at the time, which was when I really started to develop an interest in the game. I was doing three jobs at the time. I used to work in a factory, then I would weld cars for people, then I would work behind a bar on Thursday, Friday, Saturday and Sunday evenings. Darts was a great way of earning a living. Throughout my childhood and teenage years, I tried all sorts of sports. I wasn't a bad cricketer. I tried football, I tried everything, even bodybuilding for a while, but darts wasn't really on my mind at all. Yvonne (my wife) and I went out one night before we were married to the Crafty Cockney pub in Burslem, in Stoke-on-Trent, where we watched Eric Bristow on stage. He'd opened the pub there. We never used to go out at all. It must have been 12 months of living there before we eventually went to the Crafty Cockney. We would watch Eric and I said to Yvonne, "When I was young, I would have beaten him." Yvonne had never seen me play darts, even though she'd bought me a set for my birthday, which was the time I started to play with my Dad once a week. People then saw me play and I was asked to go and play for lots of teams, "Will you come and play for our team Phil?" people would ask. I was playing really well. It was such good fun. I then started to enter little tournaments, £15, £50 or £100 tournaments, and I started to win them. There'd be a tournament on a Saturday, which was £1 to enter, with £15 for the winner. That was great. I was on £4 a week pocket money at that point, so £15 on a Saturday was brilliant for me. I'd then win the £50 and £100 tournaments. I was about 26 by then. It was great as we needed furnishings for the house – we had a little two-bedroom terrace house and we either used to get everything given to us, or we would buy it second hand. So whenever I would win a tournament, the £50 or £100 would buy something new for the house: saucepans, towels, curtains, knives and forks. When we got our first duvet, it felt incredibly posh.

Who were your boyhood heroes?

I used to love watching the darts on television. It used to be on quite a lot. I would watch Eric Bristow, John Lowe and Jocky Wilson. They were household names at the time. I wasn't the biggest fan of Eric, but I did like his winning mentality. Eric was a winner; he enjoyed winning. The perfect thing would have been to have had the style of John Lowe and the winning attitude of Eric.

How did you come into contact with Eric Bristow?

It was when I started to play for the county. I was 27 at the time and we would play at the Crafty Cockney. I used to play in the Super League there and Eric had got to hear about me. That's how Eric and I got to know each other. Eric liked my attitude and my work ethic. I loved to work at it. I'd get up early and start practising. If the county matches started at 12pm, I was there at 9am. I might not start my county game until 5pm, but I'd play all day before that. I never got bored, because I could see what I was doing it for, which was to make a living for myself.

When did Eric decide to back you?

It wasn't just Eric. It was also his partner, Maureen Flowers. Eric's career was starting to go down a little, and he wanted to sponsor someone, to give him a little bit of a boost. It was late 1987, early 1988. Supporting me was like a little hobby for Eric. What he did though, which was the best thing he did, he told me that whatever money I won, I had to pay him back. In total, it was about £8,000. I had to pay him the money back, but no more – no contract, no scribbles on a fag packet, just a gentleman's agreement that he would be repaid. We never let each other down. He got his money back!

This must have been quite an exciting time for you – one of your heroes backing you and giving you confidence?

It was exciting, but it also came with a fair bit of pressure as well. At the time, I took voluntary redundancy from work to concentrate on darts full time, knowing that if I didn't make it in darts, I could return to work at a later date. I worked for a ceramics company and used to make things from clay, not just toilet handles, as Sid Waddell would say, but lots of things. I was a hand-turner. The factory has gone now. It closed down, was then knocked down and had houses built on it. So I guess I made the right decision! The work ethic that I had learnt in my jobs has never left me. I am very dedicated. I have a very one-track mind, not like the rest of the darts players. You'd never catch me in the bar.

How hands-on was Eric in his mentoring of you? How did the relationship work?

We used to practise together now and again. We wouldn't practise together all the time, as Eric found it quite difficult with me. I would drink tea or have a glass of water, whereas Eric liked a beer. He was also quite busy with his exhibition work, which I wasn't doing then. I was just dedicated and wanted to get better. Eric made me into a winner. I had to win; I had to pay Eric back. I had three children at the time, I had no choice but to go out and win. I have always kept that mindset. My parents always used to make me work. If you didn't get out of bed, my mother would chuck a bucket of water over me. By the time she had finished shouting up the stairs, you might as well have got up anyway. You knew that if you didn't, you'd get the bucket.

You were a 125-1 shot at the 1990 World Championship. What were your expectations going into that tournament?

I went in to win it. I had a tough draw with Russell Stewart in the first round, but I said to Eric that if I could get past the first round, then I could relax a little.

Having beaten Russell Stewart, Dennis Hickling, Ronnie Sharp and big Cliff Lazarenko, you came face-to-face with Bristow in the final. This must have been a strange feeling to be meeting your mentor in your first World Championship Final?

It was our collective dream really. When we used to practise together before Christmas leading up to the tournament, it was always our little dream.

Is it fair to say that winning this tournament was your big breakthrough moment?

Yes, without a shadow of a doubt. The money gave me some security. I went from having nothing to having £24,000 which was a lot of money at that time. That money allowed me to go onto the circuit properly, and I started to get sponsorships off companies. In that year, I entered 50 competitions and ended up winning 48 of them. I used to batter people. It's been like that ever since, for the best part of 20 years.

What sacrifices have you had to make in order to achieve success?

By starting darts later in life and having come from a background of having no money at all, I never wasted my money. Now I do spend money on bits and bobs, but then I absolutely couldn't. I had four kids, and I wanted them to do better in their lives. I just didn't want to waste my money, so I never went to nightclubs. Some players say that I don't enjoy myself enough. In their eyes, I probably don't, but that doesn't interest me. I'm not one bit bothered about nightclubs or casinos. I couldn't care less. That's been the story throughout my career. There may have been the odd time, when I fancied going out, but at the most, it would be three or four times a year. However, you do sacrifice a huge amount with your family. Whilst they are all growing up, you are travelling around the world. On top of the travel, I was doing four or five nights a week exhibition work as well.

If there was one piece of advice that helped you become successful, what was it?

My parents had a lot to do with it. It was bred into you. You get up and you go to work. It's your job. It's what I do. The money is a bonus, but I get up, and I do my work. I do it the best I can every time.

Do you have a set routine for mentally preparing before each match?

Yes, I do. I like to get to the venue early and normally that will be three hours before I play. I'll do my practising, sit down, have a chat, but I like to get a feel for the atmosphere, to see if it is a little chilly or not. In the three hours leading up to my match, I will practise for about two and a half hours of that. I work on getting set - getting everything right and level. It's difficult to say exactly what you are doing, but you are getting your mind right. In the case of the World Championships at Christmas time, I start to prepare for that tournament from around August time, as this is the biggest. The rest of them are good, but nothing like the World Championships. I repeat this routine wherever I play. But I also like to try things and experiment a little. I might shave a little off my flights, like a batsman might do with a cricket bat, to see if you might be able to improve just a fraction. 99% of my ideas don't work, but sometimes that 1% does, and that can make a difference.

Do you think you can control your mind?

Yes, I do. I wouldn't say that this is the case for 100% of the time though, especially when you start to struggle a little and you start to listen to every comment coming from the crowd. Nine times out of ten though, if I have prepared properly, things are fine. A couple of years ago, when I didn't prepare properly, I was looking for things to go wrong and would look to blame certain things and I would get beaten. The problem then was I was working up until two days before I was playing, so I didn't get time to practise properly. I was spending six or seven hours a day in a car, spending time in hotels, which left me short of quality practice time. Since then, I haven't done that.

What do you feel is your most destructive emotion and how do you deal with it?

I don't really have any destructive emotions. If I get any problems in my life, I can shut them out by putting a little barrier up and then I sort them out afterwards. Two weeks after my Dad's funeral, I won the World Championship. I could hear my Dad's voice saying, "Oi, get the job done." When I play now, I hear his voice sometimes. He was very quiet though my Dad. It's my mother who does all the talking.

How do you deal with doubt?

Everybody gets doubt; it's human nature. You just have to deal with it and get on with it. Experience plays a big part here. In my next game, if someone starts 180, 180, 180 against me, it doesn't matter. It's all about experience.

What do you do when you feel nervous?

I take big breaths and try to have a little break at half-time. You try and get as much oxygen as you can. But nerves come from excitement. You have to enjoy what you do. A lot of sportspeople don't enjoy it. I watch a lot of sportspeople in games and you can tell that they are not enjoying it. It's like they don't want to be there, which is weird. I love playing, 100% of the time. Even if I am under the cosh, and a few sets down, I love the chance of coming back at them. The travel is what I don't like – hours on end in a car. I don't like that.

When you are close to being beaten and you have say four or five sets to recover against an opponent, how do you go about it?

You just work at it and you have to get stuck in. I used to have hard jobs and the only way to do them was by getting off your backside and doing them. You don't think about it, you just do it. Sometimes in a game, if you look at it, you think if I take this game off him, it's my darts next and I could take the set. Then it's my darts next set, then all of a sudden, *they* are under the cosh. It's a bit like a boxing match. There are certain times when you have to hit your opponent as hard as you can.

In a big head-to-head with say Raymond van Barneveld, the lights are shining, the TV cameras are rolling, how do you stay in the zone and focus on your next three darts?

If you are playing someone good, it is a lot easier. It's easier to play against Raymond than it would be to play against you for example. I know what Raymond is going to do, so that enables me to concentrate. When I play someone I haven't played before, that can be dangerous, as my concentration may suffer, but when I am playing Barney [Raymond van Barneveld] or Lowey [John Lowe] for example, I stay consistent as I am able to concentrate. You have no choice; you simply have to concentrate. It's like fighting Mike Tyson. You know you are going to get thumped, so you might as well get on with it. That's the way I am. If I am up against a good player, then I know what to expect.

When Raymond's throwing his three darts, are you mentally relaxing waiting for your three?

I watch his darts go in all the time, so I know every score. I know exactly what he has hit, what he has left, what I have left. There are certain situations where you know that if you can hit a 180, then he is really under pressure. I don't throw three darts – I throw every dart. That's another thing I see other players do. They throw them: rat, tat, tat - which I don't. You have to make every dart count.

Have you ever suffered from dartitis*?

*a condition which can affect darts players, and severely damage their performance and results. It can be compared to the 'yips', a movement disorder which can affect golf players as they take their putting stroke.

When I was young yes, I did suffer from it, but I got rid of it quickly by throwing a house-brick onto the garden lawn like a dart.

You are an ultra-competitive person and you hate being beaten. How did you develop that mindset?

I'm not a bad loser! I don't throw tantrums or anything like that. You shrug your shoulders and then come back. Nine times out of ten when I have lost, I know exactly why. It will have been because I haven't prepared properly. I phone my sponsors up and apologise to them and they tell me not to be daft. I am not apologising for losing, but apologising for not having prepared properly. That's the one thing I cannot stand. I watch it in sport all the time and it drives me crazy. The ultra-competitive streak is already in you. If I play in people's houses, I am an absolute nightmare. Doesn't matter whose house I play in, I want to win every time. Ask Robbie Williams, he'll tell you. I'm like Jonathan Wilkes [TV presenter, actor and singer] he says, because he is dead competitive as well. Robbie can play, but he's not as good as me.

Is there anything which compares to a nine-dart finish?

It depends on where and when it is. A nine-dart finish is great. It's a great achievement, especially your first time. It's one of the best feelings in the world, especially when you get paid well for it too!

What is the best example of you being at your very best?

There was a spell once when I played Shane Burgess at the Grand Prix. It was double in, double out, and my scoring average was 126. That was me at my best, but Shane was at his best too. It was absolutely brilliant. I have moments like that all the time, but that day, it was just the whole time. In the 2009 World Championship Final, I averaged 111, but it could have been a lot better.

What's been the most important ingredient in your achieving success?

I started with nothing and I mean nothing, and I have stayed dedicated. I would get up at 6.30am, and start work at 7am, work until 4pm, come home, start welding cars until about 7pm, grab a shower, and then would work behind the bar. Not to have to do that and to be able to practise your darts with the central heating on, that's pushed me ever since, as you just don't want to go back to that.

Your career could be compared to fine wine in that you have got better and better with age. How do you stay sharp and how do you motivate yourself after so many career wins?

Age gives you the experience. As you get older, you handle the pressure better. But as you get older, you also appreciate your career more. I see youngsters on the circuit now and they regularly drink. I just can't hack that. I give them advice, but they don't listen. It's like having a puppy dog again. Every pup you have, it does exactly the same things as the pup before. I don't think these players have the ingredients to have a prolonged successful career. I don't have to motivate myself as I'm already very self-motivated. I get up and do it. There might be the odd day when I feel knackered, so I just take the day off. But that doesn't happen very often. In the past I have had times when I have had a week off, as I may have been busy running around all year, but I don't like the feeling of having to get back into training. It's like when you are fit, then you have a few weeks off and go back into the gym and think, this is awful. I don't like that.

How specifically do you practise to give yourself an edge?

I have a set routine which works for me. I know what works and what doesn't work for me. A lot of youngsters and other players don't know how to win World Championships as they don't know how to get the best out of themselves. My routine suits me. Players have practised with me in the past and said that I hardly do anything. I do though, because it is the way you practise. When I practise, I do a couple of hours, and I take it very seriously. I focus on what I need to do.

Do you 'create' pressure in practice?

Yes I do. If I am on my own, I imagine I am in the final of the World Championships playing for £1million. I'd have my opponents score in my head, and he might have gone 100, 100, 100, 100 – leave a double and finish. So you have to beat that. It's about concentration and knowing your strengths and your weaknesses. There's more to it than just walking up there and throwing some darts. A lot of it is concentration and dedication.

What percentage split in darts is talent versus the mental side of the game?

Talent is 60%, mental is 40%. Luck doesn't come into it. I don't believe the saying that you have to have a bit of luck. No, you make your own luck by working hard.

What one-line sentence would you give to anybody aspiring to be the best they could be?

Even when I said I was going to do it, people told me I was daft. They said I was crap, I was this, I was that. More than anything else, you have to believe in yourself. Don't listen to other people. It doesn't matter what anyone else says, does or thinks, you can do it yourself. And if I can do it, then you can do it; anybody can do it. It's believing that you can do it, that's the difference.

Inside and outside of darts, which sportsman or sportswoman do you admire the most and why?

That's a very difficult question for me to answer as I like a lot of players in different ways. Eric Bristow and John Lowe travelled an awful lot with a lot of dedication. I also like Dennis Priestley for his winner's instinct. But one player doesn't stand out above the others. Eric's will to win and the way he would beat his opponent made me laugh. There was so much respect in those days, the older players used to take it personally whenever anything was said. If you tried anything like that today, the players would laugh at you. That's how times have changed. If you told a player today that you'll order him a taxi, he'd just laugh at you and think you are crackers. With John Lowe and Jockey Wilson in those days, that was an insult to say something like that. There are different values today I suppose. Outside of darts, there are just so many. I like Joe Calzaghe for his dedication and will to win. I like David Beckham, as he is a hard-working bloke. I have a lot of time for him. Barry Hearn, my manager, is brilliant. He has such a winning mentality and is such a positive person. Someone like Ally McCoist; he walks into a room and the light switches on. He's got that type of personality. I also like Tiger Woods for his work-ethic.

KARL MORRIS SUMMARY

I have been very fortunate over the years to work with some great players in sport and it has always fascinated me how great sportsmen and sportswomen love to talk about outstanding players in other sports. There is one person I can think of who draws universal respect from EVERY other sport and that is Phil 'The Power' Taylor.

When the conversation brings up his name there is collective admiration for the incredible story that this man has given us over the past couple of decades. To win one world championship at ANYTHING is an unbelievable achievement; to win FIFTEEN just defies belief.

There is so much in Phil's story here that people should read again and again. It is abundantly clear here is a man who has literally dragged himself from extremely humble beginnings to the very summit of the sporting world. Due to the very nature of his upbringing, he has had a very strong work ethic ingrained into every fibre of his soul.

In some ways, the modern world is a little too comfortable for many people. It is possible to become extremely rich without being one of the very best. In years gone by, people like Phil Taylor DID have to run three jobs at a time just to survive. It is this instinct to find a better life which has driven him to become - and I don't say this lightly - one of the greatest sportsmen of all time in ANY field.

I find it absorbing to hear him talk about 'every dart must count', and how he looks at things that could make a 1% difference. It is this kind of mindset that creates the environment for greatness: to be able to look at almost every action, every endeavour, every day as being a contribution to becoming the best you can be.

It is this single-minded attention to detail which says that every day you have a choice to let the time drift by and give in to your immediate need for gratification or you make the decision to take the ACTIONS that are required to become the best you can be.

When people say 'anyone can do it' I would have to counter that argument by pointing out anyone can SAY they are going to do it. It is the rare individual who actually DOES what he says he is going to do. Think about your own life and the people you know. How many actually DO what they say they are going to do? The daily rituals make up our life's story. Are your daily rituals GOOD enough for you to become what you dream about and talk about? Re-read this section many, many times because in Phil "The Power" Taylor you have the ultimate example of a man who REALLY does what he says.

LEE WESTWOOD

Lee John Westwood was born in Worksop, Nottinghamshire on 24th April 1973 and is a professional golfer. He was educated at Sir Edmund Hillary School and Valley Comprehensive School in Worksop.

He is one of a select group of golfers who has won tournaments on every major continent, including victories on the European Tour and the PGA Tour, and was named player of the year for the 1998 and 2000 seasons. He has represented Europe in the last six Ryder Cups and is the 8th most successful European player of all time with the second highest scoring average.

He has won 31 professional tournaments and his form in Major Championships has seen him go very close to winning on three occasions where he was 3rd at the 2008 US Open, and was tied 3rd in both the 2009 Open Championship and the 2009 US PGA Championship. His renaissance was confirmed when he won the inaugural Race To Dubai in 2009, having last won the European Order of Merit in 2000. This achievement saw him crowned European Tour Golfer of the Year 2009.

QUESTIONS

You didn't start playing the game of golf until you were 13. What sparked your interest in the game?

One Christmas, I got a half-set of clubs from my grandparents. They had bought them off the guy that my Mum worked for. I put them away in the cupboard and then the next summer, my Dad, who was a schoolteacher, decided that rather than have me throw stones in the canal where he was fishing - I hated fishing and he loved it - we would get the clubs out and have a game of golf. It went from there, as we both started playing on the same day.

This must be fairly unique in golfing circles, father and son starting at the same time?

Yes, absolutely. Normally someone in the family plays, but we both started at the same time. He got down to a 12 or 13 handicap, and I was plus 5, so I have to give him a few shots now.

Within two years of taking up golf, you had become junior champion of Nottingham. How on earth did you progress so quickly? You must have been playing every other day?

I played a lot and I did a lot of practice. I obviously had some natural talent for it. Once my Dad had noticed that I had a bit of a talent for it, he booked me in for lessons straight away, so I didn't get into too many bad habits and I had the right technique straight away. The early success was driven by the coaching that I had right at the very beginning. I had junior coaching at Worksop Golf Club every Saturday morning, so I came to the lessons and just worked on it.

As a junior golfer, who were your heroes?

One of my main heroes growing up was Greg Norman. Watching Jack Nicklaus win the Masters in 1986 really set me off and got me really interested in golf. There was Nick Faldo, Bernhard Langer, Ian Woosnam, Sandy Lyle too. There was a lot of players worth watching at the time.

You won your first amateur tournament, the Peter McEvoy Trophy, in 1990, aged 17. Was this the time when you started to think you may be good enough to become a professional golfer?

I actually began to think I might be good enough when I got picked for the England Boys' team. The McEvoy was my first national win and that gave me a lot of confidence. But once I was picked for the England Boys' team, I set my sights on becoming a professional.

Three years later, you won the British Youth Championship and turned professional, just seven years after having started the game, that's some achievement.

Looking back on it now, it was a quick route to the top. It took me three years from starting the game to getting to scratch. Having got into the England Boys Team, I then won the Leaden Gold Medal, I then lost in a play-off for the European Amateur Championship. That all seemed to happen at the right time for me, so towards the end of that year I decided to turn professional. That meant that I was able to go into the professional game with a lot of confidence. It was very good timing in that respect.

Who was the biggest single influence in helping you get there?

My Dad was the driving-force early on. He took me for lessons and made sure I understood the lessons. When I went away and didn't have the coach there giving me lessons, he would say what the coach had been saying to me and he kept a close eye on me. More than anyone else, my Dad was the one who pushed me forward.

Was there a big breakthrough moment or day in your career?

No, not really. It happened over a period of time. Day by day, you build up the confidence and it's difficult to single out any individual moment.

You won your first tournament, the Volvo Scandinavian Masters, in 1996, when you beat Paul Broadhurst and Russell Claydon in a play-off. Paul Broadhurst had already won six European Tour events at the time. What was your mindset going into the play-off?

It all started off at the Italian Open prior to that event. There were times in the final round of that tournament when I had a 5-shot lead. I made a mess of it and didn't win the event. I had had a couple of chances to win before the Scandinavian Masters. But at that tournament, I felt ready to win. I felt like I had the game to win. I made a 40-foot putt to win the play-off, so that helped!

Just how difficult is it to get off the mark and win your first professional tournament and looking back, what mental qualities got you over the line?

More than anything, you have to have the belief. You have to feel that you fit in and that you belong on the circuit. You also have to have the game for it. That's the amazing thing about the young players that come onto the tour now - they go straight out there and feel as if they belong immediately, because they have done a lot of travelling and played in a lot of professional tournaments as amateurs. For me though, it was a question of building that experience up over the three years I had on the tour before winning.

What sacrifices have you had to make in order to achieve success?

I think you have to make sacrifices for everything. When you travel around a lot and dedicate a lot of time to one thing, you can't spend as much time doing other things. When you are away all the time, you lose track of friends. It's difficult to keep relationships with old schoolmates going. I'm not really in contact with many of them and that's an area you miss out on.

If there was one piece of advice that helped you become successful, what was it?

My Grandad always came out with the best one. He would say no matter what you do, work hard and play hard. That's basically what I try to do.

Do you have a set routine for mentally preparing before each round?

Not really. I am constantly thinking about the game and where I can improve. I go through a routine warming-up. Mentally, you learn how to switch on and then switch off.

Do you think you can control your mind?

Yes I do now, but you learn that over a period of time.

What do you feel is your most destructive emotion and how do you deal with it?

It's not so much an emotion, but one of the most destructive things is getting ahead of yourself; thinking about what might happen as opposed to what is happening. The secret is to stay in the present and to focus on what is in front of you.

How do you deal with doubt?

Doubt always creeps into your mind, but you have to think about other things. You think about good experiences you have had on the golf course that might relate to that particular moment you are going through.

What do you do when you feel nervous?

Enjoy it! Nerves are a natural reaction. You get nervous because something means something to you. There's nothing wrong with getting nervous, but it's how you control those nerves. Just don't let them affect you.

At the 2008 US Open, you had a putt to take you into a play-off. Whilst preparing for this putt, what was your overriding emotion – excitement at the possibility of it going in or nervous about the chance of it not going in, or was it 50/50 of both?

I think it was excitement about it going in, although it didn't!

At the 2009 Open Championship at Turnberry in the final round going down the 18th, you hit an incredible 9-iron shot from the bunker to get onto the green in two. You went for the birdie but ended up three-putting, when in fact a two-putt would have seen you into a play-off. If this exact situation was to present itself again, would you approach the putt any differently?

That's exactly the circumstance I talked about before, where you need to stay in the present rather than thinking about what other people are doing. The fact that Tom Watson had already hit the fairway, I wrongly figured that he would make par. It's easy to say, but I would probably do exactly the same thing again. How many chances do you get to win an Open Championship? At the time, I felt like I needed a long one to tie. Unfortunately, it didn't turn out that way, but hindsight is a wonderful thing and you can't second-guess yourself after the event.

Off the tee and on the fairway, you stand over the ball for between 10 to 12 seconds before hitting your shot. What are you thinking about in this time and what is your trigger for the swing to start?

I am weighing up everything that can affect the shot – the wind, the lie, where the trouble is, where you want to leave it for the easiest putt. There are lots of different things which go into the pre-shot routine. It's about how you are feeling as well. Thereafter, once you have thought about it, it is selecting your shot and then executing it.

Steve Richardson and Paul Way recently talked about how today's professional golfer has a better support-network around him or her. How important is it for a professional sportsperson to be surrounded by a good team?

I don't think all the players are surrounded by a team. It depends on what the individual puts in place. There are still people who don't work on the right things and don't put the pieces in place correctly, but you tend to find that the best players do.

You and your father seem to be incredibly close – and he follows you wherever you play. Do you draw strength from him being around you and how would you describe the relationship you have with your father?

We have a good relationship. He comes to a few tournaments, though he hasn't been to that many this year. He comes to whichever ones he can. We're good friends and I respect his opinion.

You won the European Order of Merit in 2000. In 2009 you achieved this feat again by winning the Race to Dubai. What has been the secret to re-discovering your very best form?

Hard work and having the right people around me. The hard work is a combination of all the things you do, both on and off the golf course. The gym work helps, and the work that I have done with my coach Pete Cowen recently has helped as well. What makes golf so difficult is that it is made up of so many different facets – so finding the right combination is the challenge.

What's been the most important ingredient in your achieving success?

Determination and mental strength.

What one-line sentence would you give to anybody aspiring to be the best they could be?

You have to have the belief in yourself. It's no good if anyone else tells you how good you are. You are the one that counts. You have to think you are good enough.

Which sportsman or sportswoman do you admire the most and why?

In golf, I have always been a big fan of the way Greg Norman plays. He has such charisma and he plays an attacking game.

When I was a kid, I would marvel at [Argentinian footballer] Diego Maradona for all of his natural talent. The little moves he made. He could influence a game. When he gave a dummy, he could almost send the whole of the opposing team in the wrong direction.

KARL MORRIS SUMMARY

I have had the pleasure over the years of being able to work on a few occasions with Lee Westwood. Have I been able to help him much? Did my tools and techniques make a difference? Not really. I learnt far more from Lee than he learnt from me.

I quickly recognised here was one of the most mentally tough sportsmen that I had ever come across; someone who had learnt how to use the power of his mind to become one of the world's best players.

Lee is almost stubborn in his self-belief, which is one of his greatest assets. When I did spend some time with him it was almost as if he had turned his self-belief on himself! He believed very strongly that his short game just wasn't good enough to compete at the top level. Some readjustment of this limiting belief and some work on the technical side have made Lee realise he has ALL of the game required to compete at the very highest level and any area which is lacking can be learnt and developed.

I believe that the way Lee responded to the disappointment of 'losing' the British Open at Turnberry is ample evidence of the solidity of his mental game. I do know a crucial conversation with his manager Andrew Chandler the day after the Open allowed Lee to put things in perspective and realise just how well he had actually played during that tournament and how well he had played throughout the whole year.

Lesser men would have suffered from the 'if only' syndrome, but he did what he needed to do and put the past behind him, looked forward in his planning and claimed the inaugural 'Race to Dubai' title.

One of the things I stress over and over again to players is that you don't just have a couple of sessions and 'get' the mental game. You need to keep working at your mental game-skills. Lee is honest enough to admit that he made a mental error on the last hole at

Turnberry by 'giving' Tom Watson a par four which resulted in him charging his first putt past the hole and ending up with a three-putt to miss out on a play-off spot.

The skill of staying 'in the present', which is a recurring theme in this book, is one which needs constant attention and is an area that takes up most of my work with athletes. As human beings we are constantly flipping backwards and forwards between the past and our PERCEIVED future. For you to become the very best you can be at any sport will require you to get very good at the skill of being in the moment. It is a very flippant and ignorant commentator who says 'he just needs to stay in the present' as though it is just a matter of asking yourself to do it. If you are thinking of being in the present, you are not in the present. The crucial skill is to become totally absorbed in the task at hand and the job right in front of you. To become totally fascinated by the challenge of the shot, the putt, the drive or whatever is facing you, as opposed to allowing your mind to wander forward to the possible OUTCOME of the shot. This is why great golfers place such value on a good routine, a series of steps which keeps their attention in the here and now.

We all need and would benefit from this skill in ALL areas of our lives, especially business. Just take note the next time you are in a meeting. Are you REALLY listening to the person in front of you or are you inside your own head thinking of what YOU are going to say when they stop talking? Just start to become more aware of your ability to be truly in the present. It is a skill that you get better at the more you do it. The rewards may not provide you with a Major Championship but they WILL provide you with a better experience of life.

For anyone looking for a role-model in the golfing world, you could do no better than look at and study Lee Westwood, as he is the personification of mental strength.

MENTALITY – THE SUMMARY
WHAT YOU CAN TAKE FROM THIS
BOOK AND APPLY TO YOUR LIFE
By Karl Morris

Normally, a book like this would finish with a summary detailing the '8 Habits' or the 'Secret Formula' of all of the stars within these pages. The 'guru' then informs us as to how we should all follow these principles. I think many of us are a bit tired of the latest expert telling us how it should be done and the guarantee of success if you follow 'his or her way'.

The BIG problem with this is there is no freedom in formulae. We are all individuals and rather than looking for THE way, we all need to find OUR way. If we blindly try to follow another person's success 'formula', I am convinced we will be found wanting and end up disappointed. What is very clear to me, having been involved in coaching for over 20 years, is we all need to be inspired and guided and NOT given a strict set of principles.

The more I have been involved with this project, the more it has become abundantly clear that all of these champions have followed their own path to success. Yes, there are some similarities throughout the pages, but what has struck me is that the way people make the best of themselves is not set rigidly in stone. The individual is sacred.

This is not to say we don't need help and we don't need coaching. So many of the descriptions within the book contain stories of a life being changed by a certain conversation or a piece of advice or guidance from a coach, friend, mentor or parent which has literally propelled that person forward. This is the way I personally suggest you use this book for yourself. You are literally party to a conversation with some of the ALL-time greats from sport.

As you have read these pages, not only have you been given a great story you have also been given the opportunity to find the pieces of advice and guidance that suit you personally.

Very often, I feel we remain stuck with a problem because we just keep looking within the boundaries of our known world. So, a golfer quite naturally would look for the answers to a golfing problem within the world of golf. Yet, it is sometimes difficult to fix a problem with the same kind of mindset that created it in the first place! To look beyond your own sport and be inspired by the stories and ideas from another discipline can often lead to a completely different perspective and potential solution.

We are by nature as human beings tellers of stories; our civilisation has grown collectively in part due to the wisdom passed down by story. I honestly feel this book is a story for our time. It needed to be written for this time. It is a story for the world we are currently in; a world where many, many people face great challenges and obstacles to finding success and happiness in their sport, business or life. By reading about how others have overcome great personal challenges we begin to plant the seed in our OWN mind of a future with possibilities, a future that will involve difficulty and hardship but a future which CAN be made successful by whatever our own definition of that term may be. We have seen time and time again within these pages that to be the person you dream about becoming involves failure, it involves setbacks, but with the right approach, the right MENTALITY, you too can be amazing. To create your own story is a way to inspire others and to get to your last round or last shot or last innings and know you have been involved in something wonderfully worthwhile is a great feeling.

I personally feel I have been involved in something amazingly meaningful here. I have been absorbed and inspired by the stories contained within these pages. It is my sincere hope you feel it has been worth your time and effort to read this book and that the lessons contained within it give you the tools to help you go out and do some really great things with your life and the lives of others.

ACKNOWLEDGEMENTS
By Joe Sillett

This book really has been a team effort. I am so happy that we got this project over the finishing-line as I genuinely believe that the book will inspire people, as it has inspired me. Meeting these great sports people and hearing their stories has been an incredibly uplifting experience. Without the stories, there would be nothing, so to every one of you, I thank you from the bottom of my heart. Thanks also to everyone who helped in organising the interviews. You know who you are.

I have a particular debt of gratitude to Chubby Chandler. Chubby, thanks a million for your support and your encouragement. Karl and Nadine Morris responded to the rallying-call with gusto; they have both been a tremendous source of energy, belief and impetus. They understood immediately what this book was about and have given their heart and soul to the cause. To Karl in particular, it has been a real pleasure to have worked with you on this project. By pure osmosis, I feel I have learnt a great deal from you and for that, I am very grateful indeed.

To my good friend Marcus Vaughan, who has been as sharp as a razor in providing ideas and feedback. Your input has been invaluable. Thank you Youth. I owe you.

To Mark Simpson QC, thank you for the inspirational title. It took a brighter mind than either of us to come up with it!

To Mike Simister, a great designer. I knew I could count on you Mike, and thanks for putting the book together.

To Philip Cunliffe and Christine Barnicoat, for their professional editing services. Getting the transcripts of interviews to read well and flow was no small task, and you have done a great job. Thanks for your superb contribution.

To John Hargreaves and jay Dixon for their expert proof-reading. Thank you so much for your efforts.

To Karen Wallin and everyone at Special Olympics GB, thank you for your support. I sincerely hope that this book will produce positive results for your organisation.

To my family, I cannot thank you enough. In particular, my parents Bob and Denise have always backed me – in success and failure. I am so very grateful for their rock-like support.

To my wife Sadie, thanks for allowing me the time to write this book and giving me such encouragement. And finally to my children Sammy, Emily and Heidi, I hope you will enjoy this book one day. Daddy loves you very much.